T0330014

Additional Praise for *Project Management Methodologies*

This book provides a global vision of project methodologies with a good balance between concept and implementation aspects.

Franco Martinig, Editor of *Methods & Tools,*
Vevey, Switzerland

Jason takes the mystery and offers a no-nonsense approach for any project-based organization to follow—regardless of their project management maturity. His book is an informative and readable discourse on how to improve project planning and delivery by selecting, tailoring, implementing and supporting project and development methodologies. The practical advice from this book will resonate with even the most process-averse reader.

Richard K. Faris, Cofounder and President
of Primavera Systems, Inc.

This is the first book that focuses on how to effectively select and implement a project management methodology. Charvat provides a clear and comprehensive portrait of the subject. He not only covers the essential elements of a generic methodology but shows how to select the appropriate methodology depending on project type.

Charvat's advice on what to look for in a project management methodology is right on the mark In particular, he shows the problems inherent in using a rigid methodology or any methodology too rigidly. The book is particularly strong in describing IT methodologies and showing the advantages and disadvantages of each.

Charvat provides a comprehensive checklist of best practices for implementing a project management methodology. Even more important, this is the first time I've seen anyone address the need for supporting the methodology once it's implemented. Again, his advice is right on target.

This book is just what you need to begin to set up a formalized and structured methodology.

James S. Pennypacker, Director,
Center for Business Practices

Jason has written a superb book that will be supportive of the efforts of project management practitioners. It contains excellent visuals that make the methodology easy to understand and can be immediately applied in the workplace.

Dr. Frank Toney, Director, Executive Initiative Institute,
leader of the Top 500 Project Management
Benchmarking Forum, author of 8 books

Jason goes beyond dispelling the myth of project management by providing a choice of proven methodologies and usable templates for any project! This is a must read book!

Michael E. Christie, Project Manager, South Africa

The marketplace has long needed a book like this. Methodology is the basis of successful project management. This book gives us a comprehensive overview and analysis of the methodologies available that impact our discipline.

Joan Knutson, Speaker, and executive coach,
Author of *Succeeding in Project-Driven Organizations:*
People, Processes and Politics, San Francisco

Jay brings a much needed perspective to the world of project management discussions: one of real-world experience. Where others remain ensconced in theory and what-if, Jay gives the reader an opportunity to learn how those halcyon project methodologies transform as they travel down the bumpy road to real implementations in today's organizations. I, for one, am planning to use his experiences and insight to my advantage.

Rick Turoczy, Senior Manager, Marketing, ProSight,
the experts in portfolio management software

A great addition to any developers library. It comes highly recommended.

Carl Hamilton, one of Sweden's most provocative
and original literary voices, television host,
and author of *Absolut: Biography of a Bottle*

PROJECT MANAGEMENT METHODOLOGIES

selecting, implementing, and supporting methodologies and processes for projects

jason charvat

JOHN WILEY & SONS, INC.

Published by John Wiley & Sons, Inc., Hoboken, New Jersey.
Published simultaneously in Canada.

For general information on our other products and services please contact our Customer Care Department within the United States at (800) 762-2974, outside the United States at (317) 572-3993 or fax (317) 572-4002.

Wiley also publishes its books in a variety of electronic formats. Some content that appears in print may not be available in electronic books. For more information about Wiley products, visit our Web site at www.wiley.com.

Library of Congress Cataloging-in-Publication Data:

Charvat, Jason, 1967–
    Project management methodologies : selecting, implementing, and supporting methodologies and processes for projects / Jason P. Charvat.
      p.   cm.
    Includes bibliographical references and index.
    ISBN 0-471-22178-3 (CLOTH : alk paper)
    1. Project management. 2. Industrial management—Methodology. I. Title.
  HD69.P75C46   2003
  658.4′04—dc21

                                   2002014044

Acknowledgments

Although I write alone, I do not learn alone. In large part, this book is the product of colleagues and clients I have had the privilege of working with during my project travels. The shortcomings of this book are mine. The strengths are from those from whom I have learned. Many have interrupted their busy schedules so that I might better understand the challenges of methodology design, selection, and implementation. I would like to recognize the support of the management team at RCG Information Technology, Inc., who provided me with an environment in which to apply my skills. Thanks to Brian Hurley for his review and for listening to the likes of Petronius Arbiter and to one of the best cartoonists and toy designers of our time, Bill Baron of Ranchos de Taos, New Mexico, for the cartoon used in this book. My appreciation is extended to Bob Fairchild and Mike Christie for reviewing much of my work and giving me another view on how it really works in practice. I thank the team at John Wiley & Sons, who made this all possible—Matt Holt, senior editor, and Tamara Hummel. To my parents— Frank and Peggy—thank you! To Rudy, Candy, Shelly, and Butchy—thank you for your kind words and continuous encouragement. Special mention always goes to my wife, Liesl, and son, Matthew, for their unwavering support during the writing of this book. To all those who have contributed toward the publication of this book, I thank you collectively.

Contents

Foreword

Any reader of this book undoubtedly has been associated with an IT project in distress. It is the fundamental nature of every IT project. First, IT projects are always complex with a multitude of variables. Most application implementations cut across multiple business units, each with their unique business requirements. The implementation often has differing degrees of priority, depending on the business unit. Second, a new or altered application must often interface with many other applications, thereby creating an integration challenge that is difficult to estimate in both time and resources. Worse yet, the downstream impact to these other systems may cause adverse consequences that may not be felt until long after "go live" day. Further, assigning and managing scarce resources often cause a project manager to rethink his or her chosen profession. And what about your client's responsibilities? Whether a paid external engagement or an internal business unit, your client, too, has deliverables along a project's path. Strong requirements definition, design approval, end user testing, and end user training are typical client tasks that, if not completed on time, cause schedule slippage and cost overruns. And the finger of blame usually gets pointed at the project manager.

Who among us has never been associated with a failed project? Some very extensive and well-documented surveys indicate that 84 percent of IT projects either fail outright or are delivered late. A Fortune 100 CIO once told me that an IT project is like the Bermuda Triangle: cost, schedule, quality. On a good day, you can hit two out of three, but you *never* can declare success in all three. Well, I strongly disagree!

Effective project management begins with executive commitment and sponsorship. Without the "chief" declaring a sense of urgency and importance to the project, it is doomed to dismal results right from the start. Second, it is critical that an enterprise adopt a common process and a common toolset for how projects are managed. Your company must select a project management methodology and a standardized framework for measuring progress. Then, select a toolset for project plan and milestone capture. Next, deploy a plan to educate the enterprise. Finally, aggressively communicate status with clients and stakeholders. This is easier said than done. But what I am describing is a systemic, methodical approach to making project management a part of everyday culture. When *all* projects in the enterprise follow a standardized template, then and only then will project management evolve gradually into an everyday way of life. When an organization's maturity reaches a repeatable model, management of projects becomes an institutionalized process. Hence, results become predictable. Therefore, all three corners of the Bermuda Triangle can be achieved on *every* project.

In *Project Management Methodologies: Selecting, Implementing, and Supporting Methodologies and Processes for Projects*, Jason P. Charvat deals explicitly with the manner in which project methodologies relate to organizational processes. He deals with the essentials of selecting a project framework not only for competency on a particular project, but for the entire enterprise. He also recognizes that corporations are dynamic and ever changing and instructs us, therefore, on how organizational project methodologies and processes can be maintained and supported. As he points out, "It is a rare occasion that a project process will remain the way it is."

Perhaps most important, Jason discusses the crucial role of the project office within the organization—the role of managing project methodologies and project processes in general. For an enterprise to truly make its approach to project management part of its everyday culture, the role of the project office cannot be understated.

This book ideally covers topics from simple project management templates to the challenges of implementing a common framework across an entire enterprise.

ROBERT D. SIMPLOT
President/CEO
RCG Information Technology, Inc.

Introduction

Most conferences are based on technology—gadgets or operating systems or the latest stuff—and it was during an international gadget show that I remember being asked by an attending delegate exactly what it was that we did, as he didn't see many gadgets lying around. "We provide companies with various solutions using various project management methodologies and best practices. We will help you achieve the business benefits you need, because we can bring projects within specification, schedule, and cost," I said. It has been my custom to attend as many leading-edge technology conferences and seminars as time permits, as I believe that project management can be applied to any conceivable industry and I was now hoping to provide the best answers where and when needed.

The delegate asked me a fundamental question: "Which methodology would you use in my company, as we use various technologies and platforms? Some projects are not IT-related but fall more into the manufacturing and logistics environments." I was very bluntly told to cut all the superfluous nonsense, as he'd sent many of his staff on project training and, to date, nothing much had changed! Projects were changing almost every second week. This directness amazed me and made me wonder what perception businesses had regarding project management structures and methodologies needed for companies worldwide.

Nonetheless, I invited the delegate into our meeting room to discuss some of his concerns, the projects they were managing, their technologies, and the products being produced. In a short time, I realized they had no formal project framework by which their projects were managed. It seemed that even their product development was incorrect. I subsequently illustrated a few methodologies they would most likely need. He seemed impressed and we exchanged some details. It turned out the delegate was the president and CEO of a Fortune 100 company who needed some detail surrounding project management methodologies and someone to design and deploy this for his company. The delegate was very excited about this, and we set up another series of meetings with his executive team. Within a few weeks, a purchase order was signed allowing us to implement an enterprise-wide project methodology framework, establish a project management office, and tailor his development practices for his product lines. Additionally, we included a fresh relook at the company's project templates and processes.

I realized some time later that there weren't many publications that addressed project methodologies and templates. Those that did were either too complex or extremely expensive. Information available at project conferences I attended was limited and you had to spend a small fortune to buy a generic project methodology, which attempted to solve everything. By that stage, I knew about 20 methodologies in use, but those methodologies were not well known by the project management community.

I knew something was missing and concluded that I needed to add value to the project community by filling in some or most of the project methodology gaps. This publication on project management methodologies shows various project life cycle approaches, which any newcomer or practicing project manager can work with. If you are in the construction, aeronautical, energy, education, social, government, or information technology sectors, you soon realize that there are many common factors evident throughout this book that can be universally applied to your projects. Even if it looks very IT-orientated, you can use it elsewhere.

This is a book of loosely coupled project methodologies and development strategies used by project managers today. They are coupled in that they all focus on the same broad subject—project methodology/processes. Today's leaner, meaner project organizations look to project management to provide them with a sustainable competitive advantage. That's why the project managers who are in greatest demand are those who are well versed in modern planning techniques and are capable of developing and deploying projects from start to finish, ever alert to their companies' current and future business needs. There is no time to waste after a project has been started!

This book is for neophyte managers, seasoned executives, and practicing project managers who worry that their companies will be caught flat-footed by not having a project methodology in place. I also provide advice on actions to radically design and improve the efficiency and effectiveness of current project methodologies and processes used in organizations. The word *efficiency* means the organization's productivity or its ability to productively meet the needs of any project, irrespective of the industry type and size. Every project undertaken today requires a common structure or framework in which to start these projects.

Most people, when asked to characterize the project methodology or processes they use, say that their company is either in the banking, construction, manufacturing, or information technology industry and that they use a tailored project methodology—often proprietary—that was designed specifically for their unique environment. Surely, however, there has to be some common thread between all projects! Or are all projects tailored specifically just by using only the life cycle phase components that are needed, which forms the basis for a *specific* industry? Hence, the question is: Do we have a universal project management framework or are there others we can use? There are many organizations that would profess that theirs is the only true methodology available, but sometimes it may not be suitable for their environment at all. Project managers should explore their options more closely, and they will find at least a dozen project methodologies available for use immediately. The methodology choice depends on the project type, size, complexity, duration, and organization. In this book, I present you with many options.

In my previous book, *Project Management Nation: Tools, Techniques, and Goals for the New and Practicing IT Project Manager,* I presented an introduction to this universal methodology framework, which was customized for the information technology environment. In this book, I present various methodologies that can be used by virtually every industry using project management—not just IT—as the way to achieve business goals. You will find that these methodologies work. It is my recommendation that the overriding objective of the project manager and executives must be to achieve a state of alignment between the business and the project itself. Many organizations are not aligned to project processes, and projects subsequently fail in a great many areas because of this. It is fundamental that these misaligned organizations be redesigned and reengineered—painful but necessary.

As Descartes said, "Perhaps everything we believe is wrong. Perhaps."

This book focuses on two major themes:

1. What are project frameworks and methodologies all about?
2. How do you design and implement them in your organization?

My view is framed in the idea that companies must adapt to accommodate and serve the business models of the future. My entire thrust here is, therefore, to explain how to design a project methodology and determine if the existing methodology is sufficient. In most areas, eventually everything has only a past rather than a future, so we should challenge existing project methodologies and review their advantages and disadvantages and their mannerisms and success. Organizations all use processes, project templates, and techniques to deliver and deploy projects. It's obvious and glaring that project methodologies will pave the way for the future for the next wave of organizations. Just look at innovative companies such as Nokia, Disney, Virgin, J&J, Honda, and Charles Schwab. They have proved themselves more than competent to bridge economic obstacles by having innovative methodologies and systems in place, and they are able to adapt faster than most competitors.

The past four years have been an exceptional period of intense change and excitement in the project management environment. With all this activity, however, tremendous pressure has come for organizations to get results. Businesses demand better value for their dollars. During this time, the topic "project methodology" conjured up images of a high-tech project process, which was formed in stone. Few at the time had even been exposed to a project methodology. Today, anyone with access to consulting companies and leading edge organizations knows that there are a host of dynamic project methodologies that can be used for either project development or project deployment. Likewise, the past four years have been a unique creative and changing period for me. This book provides advice on methodologies and templates for the harried project manager or executive—advice and counsel that is best described as "deep and far reaching."

The genre of project methodologies rose to prominence in the late 1990s after being introduced more formally by various project management and military organizations. However, during the past four years, various project methodologies have lived up to their initial hype, and the flexibility of such methodologies is a testament to the continuing success and growth of project management as a professional discipline. In this book, I survey the terrain of existing and emerging project methodologies and reveal how successful organizations have adapted their business strategies to this new environment—and triumphed. I define project methodologies in terms of goals, relationship to actions, and impact on organizational structure, and point out specific ways these methodologies affect the overall business plan. The most important principle is that your project strategy must be right; if it is wrong or the methodology inappropriate for the project, it is not surprising that the results are less than satisfactory.

If you are reasonably new to project management, or if you have never designed, reviewed, or followed a project methodology before, you may be wondering if this is the right book for you to tackle. Because all of the concepts in the book are illustrated with process flows, you can work your way through the subject regardless of your experience level. If you understand what phases, components, processes, and templates are, you will benefit from this book. The sort of person who might want to read this book includes you if any of the following ring true:

➤ You are an experienced project manager, understand the fundamentals of project methodologies, and would like to move up to the next level in project management.

➤ You've had some basic project management classes, have a grasp of what a project methodology is, and have heard that there are many different ways projects can be managed.

➤ You are a consultant who regularly comes across business proposals and organizations that necessitate tailored and customized approaches for solutions and projects required by the client.

If you are a beginner, the book will provide you with great insight. Project methodology is a good topic to start with and, if you take it slowly and work through all the chapters, you can pick up the concepts and start building and managing your own project methodologies. The chapters focus on the same broad subject, project management methodologies. This book originated from seminars and presentations from my consulting work at Fortune 100 companies. It was developed in response to some related observations:

➤ Could one universal project methodology model benefit all projects in existence? The rationale is that the basic building blocks of the model are relatively the same but need only be tailored to suit the organization.

➤ A vocal band of pundits, purists, oracles, and knowledgeable project managers assert that a single universal project methodology is not as practical as it seems. This eclectic group argues, often quite persuasively and with zealous righteousness, that project management is revealing that there is more than one way to manage projects.

An entire series of project methodologies exists that can be (1) selected, (2) tailored, and (3) implemented for a specific project.

All the chapters are independent, yet connected. Content includes:

➤ *Chapter 1: Understanding Project Methodologies.* This chapter is primarily for the project managers and executives who are responsible for understanding the concepts of project methodologies and processes, their relationships to projects, and, more importantly, the manner in which project methodologies relate to organizational processes. Without a clear methodology, projects can fail miserably because business objectives are not being met. In this chapter, I explore the consequences of not having a clear methodology in place.

➤ *Chapter 2: Project Methodologies Explained.* An overview of many project methodologies available in industry today is provided in this chapter. I guide the reader to recognize what a methodology is and how it allows the organization to achieve. To simply implement a project based on a process is no longer good enough.

➤ *Chapter 3: Project Management Frameworks.* Selecting a project management framework can be demanding and challenging for any project manager or executive who has never attempted to implement one. This chapter discusses the essentials of selecting a project framework for the sole purpose of establishing a core project management competency not only on a project, but also in the company. Simply put, many project failures result from not having a project framework in place. We look at ways of overcoming these failures in this chapter.

➤ *Chapter 4: Development Methodology—Selection and Utilization.* This chapter discusses using development methodologies—of which there are many—in a project scenario.

After we have covered how the overall strategy drives project management, Chapters 5 through 8 focus on what the project manager needs to do with his or her project team and stakeholders to ensure that the project goals are achieved and that the business benefits are delivered.

➤ *Chapter 5: Implementing Project Methodologies.* In this chapter, I concentrate on how to implement various project development methodologies. Project managers do not simply jump in and run with any development methodology; there are guidelines and rules to consider before the development process begins. We look at selecting and using the right development for the project.

➤ *Chapter 6: Supporting the Methodology.* This chapter explores the manner in which both project-specific and organizational project methodologies and processes are maintained and supported. It is a rare occasion that a project process remains the way it is. Changing functionality and the manner by which organizations move dictate that some aspects of the methodology need to be supported. This chapter discusses the roles and responsibilities of the support function as related to project methodologies.

➤ *Chapter 7: Project Templates and Techniques.* Crucial project templates and techniques, which are relevant to the various project methodologies, are reviewed in this chapter. Because any project requires templates for each life cycle phase of the methodology, I discuss how to identify the required templates, how to obtain access to these templates via CD-ROM, and how to use these templates for projects in a timely manner. In addition, various case studies of actual organizations that have designed and deployed their own methodologies or have used proven methodologies from consulting groups are presented. The reader is guided through the pitfalls and benefits organizations have gained from a practical perspective.

➤ *Chapter 8: Project Processes and Trends.* In this chapter, I examine the crucial role the project office plays in managing project methodologies and project processes in general. Many organizations fail to deliver even the smallest number of projects because of ineffective project office participation in project methodologies.

➤ *Appendix: Questions and Answers.* The appendix lists the end-of-the-chapter questions, along with suggested answers. The questions are relevant and controversial to the topic of project management methodologies.

This book should be of interest to both the new and practicing project managers who are interested in starting any project. Knowing key areas and which templates are needed and understanding what to do during each project phase, with the addition of valuable project lessons learned, go a long way in establishing your credibility as a project manager. My intention with this book is not to delve into the great depths of each knowledge area and techniques such as PERT and GANTT charts, but rather to supplement it from a methodology perspective. I welcome any critique you may have.

I made an exhaustive search to locate all available project methodologies and to identify their commonalities, differences, and ease of use. These methodologies ranged from straightforward to very complex; many came with a substantial price tag, or disruptive legal clauses, and, therefore, were left out. I built on this research to present personal experience and those methodologies I felt contributed to project management. Those that I did not include may be in future editions of this book. I recommend that you read as much literature as possible on relevant project management areas and process design to improve your practical techniques, skills, and abilities. To this end, this book enables the newcomer and seasoned project manager alike to discover how to design and use project management methodologies.

It is my intention to strategically analyze the situation so that a viable path to success is selected. I believe that the arguments of colleagues and peers who claim that a universal methodology is conclusive is fallacious. They demonstrate a lack of deeper thinking into the subject of project management. I also believe that a universal common methodology, although well intentioned, is simply just not good enough. If we are to maximize the benefits from the great big world of project management, we must offer a compelling logic—a logic of methodologies that are different and can be tailored for each specific project. Whether you agree or disagree with my arguments, you will surely find them most interesting, provocative, and compelling. In conclusion, we who are responsible for managing projects must do so with uniqueness and diligence, ensuring that project management will continue to be seen as the key differentiator by which organizations want to deliver products and solutions. This book is based on my experience, valuable client input, and discussions held with fellow project managers. The opinions expressed in this book are those of the author and do not necessarily represent those of other published works.

Chapter 1

Understanding Project Methodologies

Many project management methodologies used today are either the wrong methodologies or are not applied fully. Some project managers see methodologies as impractical and bureaucratic, relying on their gut instinct when it comes to managing projects. This book will reassure you of the importance of methodologies. If project management methodologies come across as too complex to use in real world projects, project managers will look for their own shortcuts. Given enough time, anyone can be trained to adhere to a project methodology. Good project management is the key throughout this book. There is no right or wrong project methodology—provided you apply it in the right situation.

Miyamoto Musashi, a seventeenth-century samurai, stated:

> One can win with the long sword, and one can win with the short sword as well. For this reason, the precise size of the sword is not fixed. The way of my school is the spirit of gaining victory by any means. . . . (p. 20)

If an organization's business is project orientated, it must master project management to be successful in the marketplace. This applies to construction, engineering, finance, education, government, information technology, or any other type of industry. The key point is: How can we build and deploy quality projects or services? Just look at Disney, Nokia, J&J, Vodafone, and Virgin as prime examples of how companies have produced phenomenal products, starting with innovative ideas, designed and built against their own project/development methodologies, and then deployed globally. What is the secret to their success? These companies used project/development methodologies that allowed them the innovativeness to deliver their projects more quickly to market than their competitors. If a methodology looks orientated to information technology (IT), you can use it effectively elsewhere, in the energy, aeronautical, social, government, construction, financial, or consulting industries.

Using project methodologies is a business strategy allowing companies to maximize the project's value to the organization. The methodologies must evolve and be "tweaked" to accommodate a company's changing focus or direction. It is almost a mind-set, a way that reshapes entire organizational processes: sales and marketing, product design, planning, deployment, recruitment, finance, and operations and support. It presents a radical cultural shift for many organizations. As industries and companies change, so must their methodologies. If not, they're losing the point (Figure 1.1).

■ WHAT IS A METHODOLOGY?

In my quest to define *methodology*, I started by asking colleagues and associates some questions with the intent of "stirring the

Figure 1.1   Cartoon showing importance of using correct methodology.

pot." I received at least 20 different definitions of what a methodology is and used only those definitions that seemed helpful. The questions I posed were: What is a *methodology?* Should there be many methodologies? Is one better than another? How would you know which phases to adopt? How can we apply these results to a project? The answers to those questions resulted in the following definition of a methodology:

> A *methodology* is a set of guidelines or principles that can be tailored and applied to a specific situation. In a project environment, these guidelines might be a list of things to do. A methodology could also be a specific approach, templates, forms, and even checklists used over the project life cycle.

A methodology can also be defined in other ways; for example:

➤ A process that documents a series of steps and procedures to bring about the successful completion of a project.

➤ A defined process for accomplishing an end.

➤ A series of steps through which the project progresses.

➤ A collection of methods, procedures, and standards that define a synthesis of engineering and management approaches designed to deliver a product, service, or solution.

➤ An integrated assembly of tasks, techniques, tools, roles and responsibilities, and milestones used for delivering the project.

A formal project methodology should lead the work of all team members throughout the life cycle of a project. All members of a team should be familiar with and use the chosen methodology throughout their projects. Many project management methodologies address the management of a single project, without appreciating that many other projects in a company compete for the very same resources and attention. The project management methodology should also provide project managers with the perspective that there is a project management framework and associated methodologies present in the company. It may be useful to think about what a project management methodology *is not:*

➤ A quick fix.
➤ A silver bullet.
➤ A temporary solution.
➤ A cookbook approach for project success.

➤ **How Many Methodologies Are There?**

There is no one-size-fits-all methodology. Some companies have methodologies that cover everything from an initial sales call to operational support, while others cover merely the aspect of design and development. Most published books discussing methodologies focus on one role—the IT community. These books elaborate on how specific IT designs should be performed, discussing a few techniques and a few drawing standards for a specific methodology. Fitting this into your company's idea of a project methodology framework is sometimes difficult to understand, impractical, and not always easy to implement.

There is an additional problem with the single universal project methodology approach. Many project managers have found that, in practice, you cannot simply use a methodology exactly as it stands. They soon realized that they needed to modify and tailor whichever methodology they selected to suit their own company project needs. They followed a "pick-and-choose" approach, using what they needed.

When examining methodologies later in this book, we see that a methodology is "larger" when it contains more elements. Because a methodology exists primarily for project managers to coordinate project team members, coordination is appropriately larger on a large project. The methodology grows proportionally to the number of roles and work product types. Therefore, we should not expect a small-team methodology to work properly for a big team, or a big-team methodology for a small team. Thus, you need to be practical about selecting an appropriate methodology.

➤ Shortcomings of Many Project Methodologies

There are shortcomings to any methodology. Before we start by describing the best way to proceed with project methodologies, we need to first understand where methodologies can possibly go wrong. In my search for the über-methodology to recommend, I realized that many project methodologies:

- ➤ Are abstract and high level.
- ➤ Contain insufficient narratives to support these methodologies.
- ➤ Are not functional or do not address crucial areas (i.e., QA, CM, testing).
- ➤ Ignore the industry standards and best practices.
- ➤ Look impressive but lack real integration into the business.
- ➤ Use nonstandard project conventions and terminology.
- ➤ Compete for similar resources without addressing this problem.
- ➤ Don't have any performance metrics.
- ➤ Take too long to complete because of bureaucracy and administration.

➤ Projects Influence Methodologies

Not one single project methodology can solve every project across all industries. For example, the Channel tunnel project linking the United Kingdom to France came with many problems and had major cost and schedule overruns. Project methodologies were developed to prevent such problems. Many project methodologies come close to preventing problems, and many are tailored to specific uses, but it finally boils down to applying solid project management principles. Methodologies affect project management; they affect any project universally in the sense that each methodology:

➤ Contains project phases.

➤ Measures progress.

➤ Takes corrective actions based on defects found.

➤ Assigns resources to various phases.

Project methodologies are useful to companies only when the tasks are appropriate and applicable. In many project studies, project plans are seldom updated. Why is this? Many projects focus only on satisfying clients during the initial deployment phases instead of conforming to the actual plan as the project proceeds throughout the project life cycle.

In Figure 1.2, we see that Project A has no methodology and is filled with process issues as well as problems that actually increase as the project moves along. Additionally, Project B, which has a structured methodology with defined and operational project processes, minimizes the number of problems that may occur on the project. I do not contend that there will never be any problems if a project methodology is in place; it does, however, mean that you have planned for all areas of the project to function while trying to meet the objectives.

In assessing any company, we see that project management (PM) methodology does not exist in isolation. Instead, there

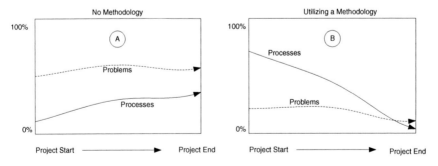

Figure 1.2 Difference in using a methodology.

are other interrelated, connected methodologies, which have a dependency on one another. Figure 1.3 illustrates that there is more than one methodology in an organization, and you need to be prepared for the one you will be using or interacting with. There is a relationship between the various methodologies, including:

➤ Sales and marketing methodology.

➤ Recruitment methodology.

➤ Project management methodology.

➤ Development methodology (i.e., specific technical build). This implies that the software or product is built more from a technical perspective than the way a project methodology is managed (e.g., when you think about building a new car, you think about the project methodology you'll be using, but hidden within the project methodology is the specific development methodology, which is precise technical steps).

➤ Operations and support methodology.

It is crucial to understand the bigger picture of what is involved before undertaking any project. For example, the fastest house builders in the world—Habitat for Humanity International—broke the world record in 1999 by building an entire four-bedroom house in 3 hours 44 minutes and 59 seconds in Auckland, New Zealand, including electrical and plumbing

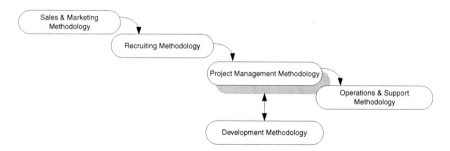

Figure 1.3 Typical methodologies used in an organization.

systems. However, the planning and coordination of this project took 14 months, which is another matter. You should not focus just on the actual "build" phase, which the record focuses on, but see which other methodologies contributed toward making this possible. Habitat for Humanity International used the following methodologies to build this house:

> ➤ A marketing methodology to market the idea to their stakeholders.
> ➤ A recruitment methodology to recruit the necessary volunteers to build the house.
> ➤ A basic project management methodology to estimate and plan this effort.
> ➤ A well-orchestrated development methodology emphasizing teamwork and multiple tasks being performed at the same time.

■ DEFINING A PROJECT

Although this book focuses primarily on various project management frameworks and development methodologies, we first clarify what a project is—a temporary effort of work, a one-time event that meets the following criteria:

> ➤ Has a start and an end date.
> ➤ Has schedule, cost, and quality constraints.
> ➤ Is a unique endeavor and contains risk.
> ➤ Has a certain scope that needs to occur.

Typical everyday examples of where we could apply a project management methodology and a development methodology include:

> ➤ The development of a new freeway as part of an existing road network.

➤ The creation of a new business unit in an organization.

➤ The design and development of a new computer system.

➤ The search for a pharmaceutical drug for a life-threatening virus.

➤ The development of a naval or space vessel.

➤ The creation of a new political party.

Project managers should realize that any repetitive continuous process is not a project. They should be focusing on a one-time event. Traditionally, a business unit decides that an organization should develop a product and turns it over to the relevant project group to establish a plan and manage the project. Additionally, the project manager must ensure that the project actually fits into the project plan that was built. Executives or clients then routinely scrutinize this plan to check for variances and request the necessary corrections or deviations. Project management thus has an important role to play. Project changes and new requirements will always be present because of legislative, regulatory, technological, or new strategic initiatives. We see why in the next section.

➤ Project Management Demystified

Before looking more closely at methodologies, we need to be aware of the key tasks that a project manager performs on any project (see Table 1.1). These are not all the objectives that you might encounter on a specific project, but the list will give you a basic feeling for what objectives are to be met.

Many companies don't have sufficient resources to perform multiple projects concurrently because of (1) turnover, (2) untrained staff, (3) unavailable staff, or (4) functional restrictions in their departments. It is important that project managers be aware of the resource commitments to other projects in their organization. A complete project management framework can determine these requirements upfront and well in advance of any crippling resource problems.

Table 1.1   Project objectives

Objectives	Responsibility	How
Obtain the user requirements	Analyst/PM, client	Interviews, URS
Define the project	PM, Client	Definition report, Business case, Feasibility study
Plan the project	PM	PBS/WBS, Gantt
Negotiate for resources	PM, Sponsor	Resource plan
Create the project team to perform the work	PM	Team contract, R&R
Execute the project, including changes	PM	Implementation plan, Change requests
Control and monitor the actual versus planned	PM	Status reports, Issue and Risk logs
Close the project and release the resources	PM, Client	Closure report
Review project and support postproject	PM, Client	Questionnaire review

➤ Project Management Responsibilities

Throughout the life of any project, project managers are responsible for the key areas. Some of these responsibilities, which tie in directly with any project methodology, follow:

- ➤ Obtain approval for the project to proceed.
- ➤ Determine the project scope and its feasibility to the overall business.
- ➤ Ensure the necessary project resources are identified and allocated.
- ➤ Plan the project to the relevant detail it requires.
- ➤ Ensure that the project methodology and associated processes are adhered to.
- ➤ Monitor the project in terms of cost, quality, and schedule.

➤ Identify and monitor project issues and risks.

➤ Provide updated reports and summaries to key stakeholders.

➤ Provide leadership to the project team.

➤ Status of Projects Today

Across all industries—whether IT or construction—we are encountering many of the same problems time and time again, irrespective of geographic location. I have heard project managers in China, Brazil, Amsterdam, and Munich complain bitterly about similar issues on their projects. Problems such as cost and schedule overruns, poor sponsorship, no user involvement, and many other problems are encountered daily. These project managers either don't use their project methodologies effectively or don't use them at all. Project management is not simple; our primary role is to resolve or eliminate daily challenges. We now examine some of the universal challenges facing project managers, which are listed in Table 1.2.

Table 1.2 Challenging project issues

Challenge	Questions Facing Project Managers
Competition gaining ground	How do we develop projects faster than before?
Constantly changing requirements	What do we need to meet both project and client needs?
Larger and more complex projects	How do we ensure quality is built into our projects?
Inaccurate designs	How do we ensure our methodology captures an effective design?
Ineffective documentation	How do we know which templates to use per project type?
Inadequate resources	How do we address resource requirements and plan for them?
Postproject support	How do we address handoff of our project to operations?

■ WHY DO PROJECTS FAIL?

One of the best project management oracles of all time—Dr. J. Davidson Frame—states that projects fail mainly because of two reasons: (1) a failure of estimation and (2) a failure of implementation. The following are reasons projects fail:

➤ Initial cost and schedule estimates are not revised when more information becomes available as the project progresses.

➤ Plans are not used correctly or used to guide the project forward.

➤ Project managers are not trained to acquire the necessary skill base; subsequently, the same mistakes are made repeatedly.

➤ The theory of project management is not put into practice. This point can be seen in the attitude of many managers who view theory as a waste of time—yet time is found to repair errors later. Isn't that a sure sign of the wrong approach?

➤ The project scope changes.

➤ The incorrect project methodology is used.

➤ Requirements have major changes.

➤ Communications are poor.

➤ Testing and/or inspections are poorly done.

Figure 1.4 shows familiar issues that cause problems on projects. However, any problem can be resolved by carefully drawing a problem matrix. If we have a project that is "over schedule," we can follow this through on the matrix and see that it was caused by a "waterfall approach." The solution to this problem is selecting an iterative methodology.

➤ Examining the Need for Methodologies

Today, projects require much tighter integration and innovativeness than what we have seen during the past decade; this

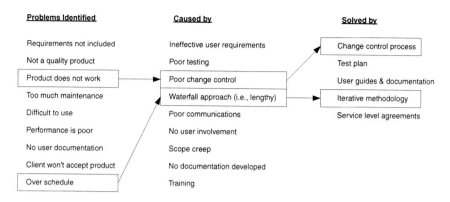

Figure 1.4 Problem resolution and fault-finding technique.

alone necessitates the use of more creative ways to design, build, test, and deploy products and services. A manager can no longer create a project schedule by filling in one or two templates. Companies require more out of their projects than ever before. One way to achieve a more efficient result is to adopt newer, swifter, and "lighter" project methodologies. Gone are the days of using a bureaucratic life-cycle approach, unless you have a very simple project that requires serious coordination and control. Table 1.3 shows us that project managers and executives have to be innovative and creative if they want to resolve historical problems.

Companies are increasingly looking to project management teams to provide solutions to many of the challenges listed previously. Methodology can assist in the sharing of information across a "virtual project enterprise." Projects have significant technical, resource, and data components that require management through their life cycle. Projects must comply with the correct standards and guidelines to protect the users' investment in such systems.

How do we select a comprehensive project management methodology that is very useful to anyone managing projects? A methodology that can be applied to a cross section of industries can be customized to reflect a specific project environment in an industry. When implementing a project, a multitude of areas should be investigated to determine what course of action to

Table 1.3   Drivers for using methodologies

Reasons for Change?	What Do We Want to Change?
Shorten project schedules	Improve the planned schedule.
Reduce project costs	Improve the overall project profits without affecting quality.
Be flexible on project execution	Adjust the project within the boundaries.
Improve customer support	Address client needs.
Be able to fast-track projects	Perform common tasks simultaneously.
Increase project quality	Introduce quality and testing from day one.
Improve client participation	Improve requirements gathering and client participation.
Constant changes	Reduce constant change by defining a change process.
Unpredictable results	Have repeatable results and be able to measure performance.

pursue. The many variables that require management in the complex environment also represent areas that can be exploited to achieve productivity and cost advantages during project execution.

Projects have definite life cycles that determine how the projects are actually managed from the initial discovery phase through detailed design, construction through to the delivery, and eventual operation of the product. The secret to the success of any methodology is this: It uses solid, repeatable processes that serve as the foundation for any successful project initiative, supported by sufficient documentation and relevant processes providing (1) repeatable best practices, (2) consistency of results, and (3) a quicker path to results.

Project managers often ask: "How can we speed up the development or execution process?" Many times, they see the process as slow and painful with too many policies and procedures. The answer is either (1) by selecting a more agile methodology or (2) by cutting back on your heavyweight methodology to make up lost time and cost. Have you ever heard key staff say: "We considered developing our own methodology, but we rejected that idea after not being sure what methodology was right for us"? The best answer is to first look at your overall company strategy.

■ STRATEGY WITH METHODOLOGIES

For any company to be world class, the strategy is clear—survey the entire landscape and then put the objectives—*the what*—into a game plan—*the how*. In negative economic times, always remember that what comes down must come up. If you have formulated the right strategy and can execute (i.e., project management/development methodology), you will most likely succeed at improving the bottom line. Remember that many executives look at whether you are adding to or taking cash from the company coffers.

For example, assume a fixed price project has been awarded to Company ABC, which could possibly bring in about $1 million in revenue. Unfortunately, Company ABC doesn't adhere to any formal PM methodology, and instead relies on the project manager's experience to meet project objectives. However, the project is soon bombarded by constant change and new requirements by the client, and Company ABC realizes after a few weeks that it is losing dollars that it wouldn't have if the project manager had adhered to a PM methodology using the appropriate project templates in the concept or design phases.

In addition to having the best product or service, companies need to think about deploying innovative concepts to get their products and services to market more quickly than their competitors can. A delivery methodology is the key. Look at some examples of strategies where companies used project/development methodologies:

> ➤ You are able to go to Morpheus or Kazaa Web sites and download or purchase single music MP3 files instead of going to the local music store, where you have to purchase a complete CD with multiple music tracks that you may not want.

> ➤ You can both order and customize your Dell computer directly online through Dell Direct instead of purchasing

directly from a supplier. Their flexible product lines and ease of use gives Dell a huge competitive edge.

➤ Virgin One has a dynamic Web experience where you can bank directly using their Virgin One Account. You need only one account instead of multiple accounts for checking, savings, mortgage, credit, and so on. Virgin has proven that it can save 8 out of 10 people thousands of pounds sterling and reduce paperwork through this innovative strategy. Virgin is setting the benchmark standard for banking.

➤ Boeing is redefining its strategy from commodity-driven (aircraft engines) to service-driven. Boeing Company monitors aircraft (flight hours) and its engines in the air, literally extending this concept into multiyear contracts with British Airlines, USAir, and Southwest.

Project/development methodologies are not just about focusing on product life cycles, but also about shortening any strategic life cycles a company may have. No matter how efficient your company is, you need to adapt and you need to do so constantly.

Bill Gates has stated, "Microsoft is always two years away from failure." He's really saying that Microsoft needs to understand the reality of competition. The bottom line is "How are you going to make the jump?" Whatever your industry—be it IT or not—trends have shown that it will likely take a total newcomer with a radical approach to show you how quickly you should move. Just look at the example of how Richard Branson's Virgin group got into banking. It wasn't their immediate field of expertise, music, but they had the innovation and ability to break into an industry, which used formal "heavyweight" methodologies. Try extending this same concept to your own industry and identify newer ways of doing business. Do you think there's an outdated methodology or something missing that you would change?

For a clear, concise snapshot of my point, review Figure 1.5. It illustrates the macro view of how Company ABC—in the center—is driven by an effective strategy (A) and then proceeds

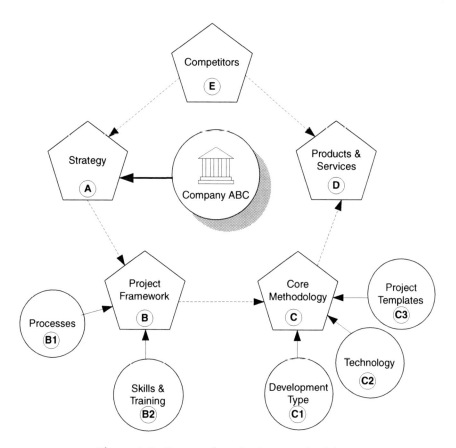

Figure 1.5 Strategy for selecting a methodology.

putting the strategy into tactical perspective by first having a project management framework (B) in place, which is fueled by its supportive processes (B1) and project skills training (B2). After this is in place, a core project management methodology is needed (C). Additionally, this is dependent on the development needed (C1) and the technology (C2) you will be using, as well as the project templates (C3) that are thought helpful. When completed, the company is free to proceed to deliver its products and services (D) to the marketplace before any of its competitors (E) do.

➤ Project Framework versus Development Methodology

There is a distinct difference between a project framework and a project methodology. The framework has always meant the various segments of the project and the development methodology are the means of getting from segment to segment. The following metaphor helps solve this subtle difference: If the project framework is seen as the "skeleton" of a building, the "floors" are seen as the different development methodologies allowing you to get through the building. Some get you there more quickly than others would.

Projects vary widely, depending on the size of the company, the size of the solution, the number of project staff assigned to the project, whether the testing is conducted in-house or in test labs, and so on. The question then arises as to what exactly project methodologies should offer us? Table 1.4 lists some of the most beneficial offerings of a good project methodology.

In other words, after identifying and selecting the correct methodology, it may be the best defense if you want to:

➤ Avoid mistakes.

➤ Reduce cost.

➤ Reduce risk.

➤ Meet project schedules.

➤ Identify and correct errors early.

➤ Avoid excessive documentation.

Many project managers are faced with developing products within a specific time with limited resources. Adopting an incorrect methodology or having no project framework in place can very easily cause you to have schedule and cost slippages, as well as miscommunication within the team. Some methodologies consume many hours, and you must follow project templates and processes, making the daily execution of the project difficult. Selecting the correct methodology allows you to develop a saleable "fit to sell" product within the correct time frame, forcing you to focus on the most appropriate documentation

Table 1.4 Benefits offered by a project methodology

Benefits We Achieve	Allows Us To
Better process	Define processes and introduce improvements.
Flexibility	Adapt from project to project.
Integrated metrics support	Gather metrics during the project.
Quality focus	Ensure that all areas of quality are addressed.
Managing complexity	Manage complex situations.
Proper project documentation	Complete critical documentation per approach.
Standard approach	Provide all projects with a common approach.
Consistency	Deliver projects using a similar approach.
Containment of all project phases	Reassess the project per phase.
Project planning	Better plan projects.
Ability to get the job done	Guide the team to completion by the various phases.
Elimination of crises management	Reduce or eliminate any crisis.
Ease of use	Easily use and implement.
Knowledge	Review and improve future projects.

and processes, without wasting time on administrative tasks that have no purpose. You do not have to use the most detailed processes. But how do you know which methodology is right for you? It's like trying on a pair of shoes—you have to select the right size, color, make, and style. We examine this question in detail in Chapter 3.

➤ Understanding Methodology Trends

Some of the most common questions that arise on the topic of project methodologies are:

> ➤ Do we honestly say that we understand the working of a basic project management methodology?

➤ Do we understand why the various project management methodologies differ?

➤ Why does the life cycle vary between project types?

➤ What does this tell us about the generic practice of project management?

If technology managers repeatedly tell us they need more time to plan the implementation and that they should have used fewer tools, hired more outside consultants, and allowed more time for training users and retraining staff, what does it tell us about our project? It tells us that the project planning was inadequate and that, most likely, the project methodology was not followed correctly.

Instead of following a standard methodology for conducting projects, many companies have been relying on technical wizardry to get projects done. In fact, communication is often so bad that it outweighs their tool-centric approach to managing the project. This leads to project management burnout. Project management is not about deadlines; it is about tracking, controlling, and improving the process of change. Lack of time may be the excuse, but why isn't the initiative planned more carefully? Perhaps it is that organizations compelled to reengineer their business processes don't have the luxury of time due to the amount of projects being undertaken by organizations as well as the speed-to-market factor. Are competitive pressures so intense that project management succumbs in the triage of crisis management?

The methodology process itself is sometimes part of the problem because when you start fiddling with the building blocks of your business, projects take on a life of their own. Therefore, an assessment of the business components must be brought into a more realistic relationship with the methodology that is going to be used. The relationship among these variables is often not linear, and this needs to be noted.

Perhaps we all have unrealistic expectations of the power of technology and the human dynamics of change. No matter how rapidly business requirements shift and technologies improve, some steps in project management cannot be combined. To keep a project methodology in sync with reality, learn from those who have gone before you. Brian Hurley, founder of Musk industries succinctly defined the situation: "Deliver your projects as you would a newborn. Conceive decisively. Gestate, prepare and then again. Don't bash your ship on the siren of complacency. Procrastination will lure you past your due date, and no late-stage boom in the headcount of gestating mothers will hasten the outcome" (p. 15).

➤ Strategic Focus

Strategy always comes before any tactics. It's similar to thinking before doing. The strategy must be correct before we select a project or development methodology. In other words, you must be doing the right thing and only then can the necessary tactics support that newfound strategy. (It's like executing a certain methodology only after we know what our objectives are.) Strategy—as it has always been and will always remain— is the perpetual struggle for advantage. The objective of strategy is to take actions that build, sustain, and compound advantage. Acquiring and retaining customers are functions of your advantages. Parrying competitors is a function of your advantages. Competitive organizations that parry with their competitors do so in order to understand their competition, allowing them to understand, maintain or build leaner, quicker processes, eventually coming in earlier to market with better products.

History proves that the best strategy and tactics are achieved in areas fundamental to the core strengths of the company (i.e., having a project management discipline). With the right strategy, the battle is only half won; the strategy succeeds only with professional execution of tactics. Many problems arise when planning is separated from that execution. The important thing is to get started. Too much time spent on planning is also not good. You get caught up doing so much planning and strategizing that you never move forward—you end up wasting time on planning and that breeds indecisiveness and error.

It is often better to engage in some form of simultaneous planning and implementation (e.g., this is where concepts such as RAD, OO&D, and concurrent engineering make huge impacts on project executions). A common mistake is to consider planning as only a mental process, an idea in our heads that looks at the past and adjusts to the future. If your plan is not in writing, you really don't have a plan at all. A simple written plan works best.

The purpose of strategy is to provide rapid direction and concentration of effort as organizations continually strive to improve their position or gain the upper hand in the marketplace. Speed is the ultimate factor here. Throughout history, winning generals developed ways and means of moving faster than their opponents. Napoleon's troops marched at 120 paces per minute while his opponents marched at only 70 paces. Because Napoleon's troops marched almost twice as fast as his opponents' troops, speed gave him a tremendous advantage, which was a major contributor to his success. Using this analogy, project managers also need to use a methodology that is not only faster than the competition, but also that is disciplined enough to ensure that the products or systems are developed, tested, and implemented properly. Figure 1.6 depicts two scenarios. The left side shows an organization faced with an unprofitable situation—the strategy is not correctly aligned to its portfolio of projects. On the right-hand side of the illustration, we see an organization that has undergone an assessment; as a result, its objectives are aligned to its project portfolio.

➤ Strategy versus Methodology

Projects of varied size and complexity require different project management skills and techniques to effectively and economically manage project risks. Shareholders now and in the future demand results, which means that companies must be innovative in how they get their products to market; they must use efficient methodologies, concepts, tools, and techniques.

Project management stands out as the enabler to make this happen. Identify the project management disciplines and techniques you would need to send some people to Mars and back. The answer: You would need them all. The challenge for most project environments, however, is to tailor or scale the methodology so it makes sense for projects of lesser size, risk,

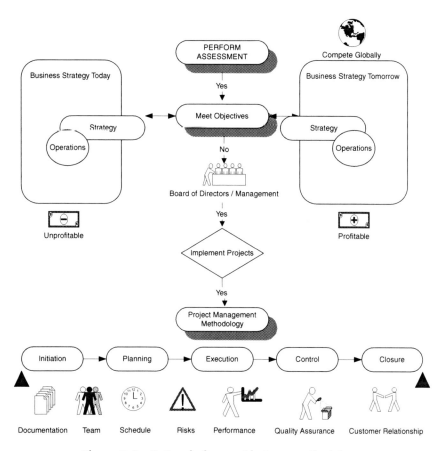

Figure 1.6 Rationale for considering a methodology.

and complexity. Additionally, project management methodologies can be thought of as a set of principles and techniques for controlling project risks, quality, change requests, and for capturing any opportunities as projects are brought to fruition. Because of economics and common sense, project management techniques need to be tailored to the specific risks and opportunities of each project. The methodology provides a means for selecting the degree of project management attention appropriate for your particular project.

You may encounter projects in which the apparent risks are so small in certain areas that, while those areas should be monitored, no formal project management techniques may be needed. In these areas, you should simply use good business management practices. For example, with an internal project whose resource needs consist of three people working for a year, you might forego a written cost estimate or cost controls because the costs would be inherent in the allocation of labor. Using elaborate or even simple cost tracking systems in such a case would be a waste of time and money. The point of project management is not to drive up your overhead or to require mountains of administration. Project management provides a set of structured techniques to help you think about project goals and risks; helps you define, structure, organize, and plan your project; and enables you to effectively monitor and control your project as it progresses toward completion.

The traditional ways of thinking about strategy and how to build advantage are no longer working. Executives need a fresh strategic imagery and analysis of how to cope with the virulent hyper competition and a prescription of how to build advantage in this new environment. How do they do this? Look at Harley Davidson's return to fame from a near collapse. Today, their production lines produce some of the best roadsters. Improved processes, as well as cutting administrative burdens, have done well for the company.

You can buy many things—technology, advice, assets, and, often, even time. What you cannot buy is commitment. Commitment is something that is earned and must be won. It is something that must be planned for and managed. The absence of commitment, not the poor selection of technology, is often the primary cause of strategy failure on a project. As hyper competition defines the competitive landscape into the new millennium, the basis of advantage will be the agility of project management methodologies. This important insight must be acted on. This insight ultimately separates the winners from the losers and the successes from the failures.

➤ Why a Project Methodology?

Many companies today do not use any formalized project methodology. They run their businesses as they always have. However, the business and technology landscape is changing rapidly. Business today calls for dynamic methodologies and processes, gearing companies to reinvent themselves so that they can produce products and services faster than ever before. Additionally, being able to produce gadgets of the right quality and specification is key. How does a company change virtually overnight, to become a company that can deliver such gadgets for their clients? Jim Highsmith of Agile Software Development Ecosystems (Addison-Wesley, 2002) states: "In a world of constant change, traditional, rigorous software development methods are insufficient for success" (p. 22).

The secret to success is the project-based company. With this comes certain provisos:

1. A set of flexible project management methodologies.
2. Processes that can be updated to support these methodologies.
3. Resources that need to be aligned with the methodology.
4. Business functions that need to support these projects.

If you are not efficient or not getting a quality product developed in time or to specification, you need a new project methodology.

➤ Selling the Project Methodology to the Company

You feel it in your bones. You're excited about a new project methodology, and you'd like to propose this new way of managing projects to your company executives. However, you hesitate to move forward because your neophyte boss, who has a black belt in corporate politics, doesn't like the idea. What should you do?

First, sell the idea to as many people as possible and never give up. It is crucial that companies needing a project or development methodology and all of its associated processes understand that if it doesn't exist, a methodology will have to be developed from scratch, purchased from a third-party vendor, simply obtained from a mutual friend in the business, or tailored from existing processes.

However, before you can do anything, you need to sell the idea to company executives, who are often unfamiliar with project management, especially a new methodology that would affect virtually the entire way their company does business. A typical response to you might be "Goodness gracious, are you mad? We've been doing business like this for years, why change now?"

A strong selling point for investing in a solid project methodology is that the greatest return on investment (ROI) lies exactly there. Few people can counsel corporations on how to identify and nurture business drivers such as brilliance, inventiveness, and thought breakthroughs. However, we can make sure that gleaming opportunities are not squandered in their subsequent development and implementation. For innovative ideas to bear fruit, sound project management principles must be followed. Maybe project managers or executives trying to sell the concept to their organizations should emphasize this feature.

Following the success of the Prussian Army in the Franco-Prussian War, the British General staff sent a team of aristocrats to find out the secret of success. They reported that all the Prussian troops were clean-shaven with short-cropped hair. The British Army accordingly copied this. Although there was no evidence that this helped their performance, it remains a law to this day—except for special duties. The moral of this story is: You can copy from others but be cautious. Don't copy the wrong thing (i.e., don't copy a methodology if it doesn't meet your needs).

■ UNDERSTANDING ORGANIZATIONS

In 210 B.C., Petronius Arbiter wrote, "We trained hard, but it seemed that every time we were beginning to form up in teams, we would be reorganized. I was later to learn in life that we tend to meet any new situation by reorganizing; and what a wonderful method it can be" (Roman author, The Satyricon, 210 B.C.). Many projects are instigated from the top down. Just look at how Toyota has turned its organization around and created product lines using efficient project methodologies and processes to become a virtual powerhouse. Toyota produces one of the best-selling cars in America. Every other auto manufacturer has tried to replicate this turn around.

Harley Davidson's organizational chart has three overlapping circles—a Create Demand circle responsible for marketing and sales, a Produce Products circle for engineering and production, and a Support circle for all other functions. However, where these three circles intersect is a Leadership and Strategy Council that oversees general management functions such as planning and budgeting. This overlapping of the circles emphasizes the interdependency between areas that encourage participation and growth.

Executives and project managers who need to understand how projects are going to be managed in the organization should first understand the company structure. Figure 1.7 shows three main types of organizational structures you might encounter when managing projects. First is a matrix structure, which is extremely difficult to work in, where project coordination and follow-up is mandatory. Second is the functional structure, which relies on the functional managers to manage their projects. Third is the projectized structure, or the project approach, which has the ability to rapidly formulate the project team and move forward.

■ LESSONS LEARNED

The following lessons learned are crucial in understanding project management methodologies:

1. Sometimes, it is not feasible to adopt another methodology and reintroduce it into your current environment. A thorough assessment and gap analysis needs to be performed before implementing such a methodology.

2. Don't try to sell a Rolls Royce to an organization that requires only a Jeep. Sometimes they really don't need all the flash.

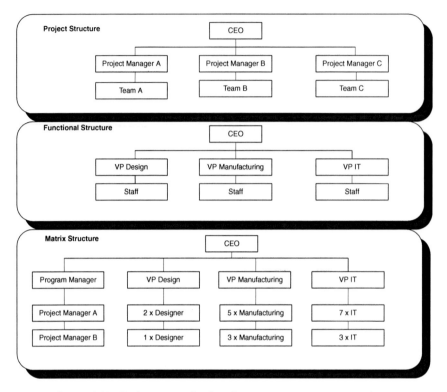

Figure 1.7 Various organizational structures to manage projects.

3. Gaining executive support for moving ahead with a project management methodology is paramount to the success of any organization. Without executive support, it becomes increasingly complex and time consuming to sell the idea of project methodology.

4. Determine your business strategy first, and then focus on the tactics you wish to employ.

■ QUESTIONS

1. Define the concept *methodology*.

2. List five shortcomings of a project methodology.

3. Apart from a project management methodology, what other methodologies would be considered relative to the project?

4. What do we mean by *project management methodology* and *project framework*?

5. What does the term *project strategy* mean? Is it the same as a business strategy?

6. How would you explain the benefits of adopting a project methodology to your client or organization?

7. Does the type of organizational structure affect the efficiency by which projects are managed through the methodology?

■ REFERENCES

Fowler, Martin. "The New Methodology." Available from www.martinfowler.com.

Hamel, Gary. *Leading the Revolution,* HBS Press, 2000. p. 56.

Highsmith, Jim. *Agile Software Development Ecosystems,* Boston: Addison-Wesley, 2002. p. 22.

Hurley, Brian. *Ispeak,* October 2002. Musk Industries, Raritan, NJ, 2002.

Michaelson, G. *Sun Tzu, The Art of War for Managers,* Adams Media, 2001. pp. 7, 14.

Musashi, M. (T. Cleary, Translator). *The Book of Five Rings.* Boston: Shambhala Publications, 2000.

Chapter

Project Methodologies Explained

■ PROJECT METHODOLOGY OVERVIEW

Key decision makers must often determine whether a universalized project life-cycle methodology is sufficient for all their projects. The answer to that question is an unequivocal no! Very few people are capable of creating a state of-the-art, concisely defined, phenomenally small, highly prescriptive, measurement-intensive, fast, and cost-efficient methodology allowing project managers greater performance improvement (consisting of an expertly designed/optimized family of policies, procedures, plans, specifications, forms, logs, and metrics). Every company has its own process flow diagram. This flow originated from a methodology created to ease implementations of new technologies or new project ideas. These process flow diagrams have many different stages, all similar in nature.

Even dynamic project-based organizations such as Accenture, KPMG, Deloitte Touche, RCG Information Technology, Bechtel, and Keane are far more than a collection of individual projects. If that were all they were, they wouldn't be multimillion-dollar organizations. They all use various arsenals of project methodologies for each solution they undertake. Companies are becoming very much like small film studios. Each project is a "movie" all by itself and has its own "director" and "script." The movie needs project funding to begin and is short lived; project teams are also short lived, and, amazingly, in this brave new model, they follow a unique project methodology, because if they don't, no one will invest in a "movie" or project. Therefore, projects need to be innovative, they need process, and they need to adhere to the "script" or methodology. Each movie script is different from the next; this is where we focus our efforts throughout the book.

By simply assessing those project methodologies that exist today, we see that a universal project approach simply won't work. The main reasons that a single "be-all-and-end-all" methodology won't work from industry to industry are differences in:

➤ Life cycle.
➤ Market sector.
➤ Product.
➤ Size.
➤ Technology.
➤ Situation.

For instance, a nuclear plant or space shuttle project has very specific heavyweight life-cycle components (e.g., work breakdown structure, activities, tasks, task durations, priorities, skill sets, and economics) compared to a small construction project. In other words, they use different phases and activities on their projects (i.e., communications and navigation equipment, operating systems, and a variety of technologies).

In addition, the life cycles for construction projects (e.g., bridge building), compared to information systems projects (e.g., three-tier architectures), may be vastly different from one another. This means much tweaking is needed if you have to accommodate every kind of project. Hence, different methodologies are needed. Therefore, we have a catch-22 situation— various technologies and industries make it very challenging to design a one-size-fits-all project life cycle. It does not seem likely that an individual project manager or executive can actually design a highly operational, functional project methodology that meets the needs of every single project—irrespective of its technology or industry. Hence, some creative genius is needed to bridge this gap. A project life cycle is, therefore, a collection of project phases. Project phases vary by project or industry, but some general phases include:

➤ Concept.

➤ Development.

➤ Implementation.

➤ Support.

Remember that products also have life cycles. Many companies have project managers or executives who are unwilling to follow systematic project methodologies all of the time. Instead, they tend to rely on standard business activities to get them through the project. They are simply trying to keep up with all this talk of project methodologies and associated processes and techniques. Questions such as "Why are there so many methodologies?" and "Which one do we use?" often arise. Over the years, even those involved in managing projects have observed that projects have common characteristics that can be formalized into a structural process, which allows them to manage projects more effectively.

Each phase can typically be brought to closure in some logical way before the next project phase begins; and each phase results in discrete milestones or deliverables, which provide the starting point for the next phase. Project methodologies should be structured to take advantage of the natural phases that occur as work progresses. The phases should be defined in terms of schedule and specific accomplishments. Define how you will know when you have finished each phase and what you will have to show for it.

Cost and schedule estimates, plans, requirements, and specifications should be updated and evaluated at the end of each phase, sometimes before deciding whether to continue with the project. At times, you may want to hold off or cancel the project. Large projects are usually structured to have major program reviews at the conclusion of significant project phases. These decision points in the life of a project are called *major milestones.* Figure 2.1 shows how project phases are somehow linked to one another. This is the basis of how project phases, once incorporated, form a typical project development methodology.

Milestone decisions are made after conducting a major program review in which the project manager presents the approved statement of requirements, acquisition strategy, design progress, test results, updated cost and schedule estimates, and risk assessments, together with a request for authorization to proceed to the next phase. The early project phases tend to shape the direction for all further efforts on the project. They provide requirement definitions, evaluation of alternative approaches, assessment of maturity of technologies, review of cost, schedule and staffing estimates, and development of specifications.

A relatively short-term or technically straightforward project may have only a few basic milestones or deliverables following a (1) proposal, (2) feasibility study, or (3) business case. Nevertheless, the project manager should report to clients and executives at intervals to keep them up-to-date on project progress, thus ensuring project direction. (See lightweight methodologies in Chapter 4.)

On small projects, if no formal agreements are written, the project manager should deal with clients and executives in an informal, yet somewhat structured and logical, manner. This

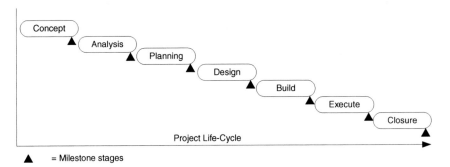

Figure 2.1 Depiction of general project methodology phases.

means managing expectations and making clear agreements about what will be produced and when. You simply cannot do this on the fly.

On long-term projects, you may find project phases take place over many months or even years, and, in this case, it is vital to provide interim deliverables to give the clients and executives a sense that work is being accomplished, to provide an opportunity for feedback, and to capture project successes in documented form. This is exactly why a project methodology works. How else are you going to do this? (See heavyweight methodologies in Chapter 4.)

It is wise that the project processes be built around the specific project methodology. Particular care should be given to defining the work to be accomplished in each phase. This should include definition of the deliverables to be produced, identifying testing and demonstrations to be completed, preparing updates of cost and schedule estimates, reassessing risks, and conducting formal technical and management reviews.

■ BACKGROUND TO PROJECT METHODOLOGIES

Project management has grown from the early initiatives in the U.S. defense and aerospace sectors in the late 1950s and 1960s. The U.S. Department of Defense and NASA achieved early project management successes—mainly promulgated through their internal policies, procedures, and lessons learned. From this flowed numerous white papers, articles, seminars, and training programs that expanded the project management genre, although much of the theory centered around the use of tools and techniques, such as:

➤ PERT/Gantt charts.
➤ Critical path.
➤ Scheduling techniques.
➤ Organizational issues.
➤ Conflict management and others.

From the early 1970s, project management societies began to provide communication on the discipline, basically through journals, conferences, and seminars. This continued until the mid-1980s when, first, the U.S.-based Project Management Institute (PMI) and, later, the U.K.-based Association for Project Management (APM), embarked on programs to test project management professionalism. This brought about certain guidelines and bodies of knowledge (e.g., PMBOK, APMBOK), which addressed some methodology but did not address every industry and type of methodology. Other organizations developed their own versions of a project methodology.

In the pioneering days of project management, it was common practice for project staff or managers to devise their own methods of moving through the life cycles of their projects, which were often influenced by information technology, engineering challenges, or financial constraints. It was a time when a project was driven by the events that occurred while on the job. This was fine for certain projects, but it led to the failure and delay of many projects because of problems that started to show (1) poor or inconsistent project designs, (2) poor project analysis, and (3) ineffective project communications. It seemed projects lacked the rigor and key ingredients to make them more effective. Sometimes, it takes a complete outsider to show how to expedite projects more quickly than before, in innovative futuristic ways. Look at what BMW has done—you can today log onto their Web site and purchase a customized vehicle, specified by you instead of selecting one from a standard showroom floor model. The production-to-delivery process is drastically reduced and flexible.

A great analogy of the need for appropriate control is found in Formula One racing. Here, the powerful cars have braking systems to enable them to go faster rather than to slow them down. Likewise, in different industries, appropriate levels of control allow an organization to grow and flourish within appropriate boundaries. Both project managers and executives need to understand the impact that new developments in technology are having on business from the project, operational, and risk points of view. It is possible to split the responsibilities of methodologies into three broad areas:

1. Managing project performance.
2. Managing the project life cycle.
3. Managing the resources and communications aspects.

Having the right processes in place to address these areas is a challenge faced by every project manager. I address each of the components of the guidelines because I believe they provide a well-researched and practical solution to this project management challenge.

Everywhere I go, clients ask the same question: "How do our project practices compare with those of our competitors or with those of our peer organizations?" Until now, this information could be obtained only from consultants, market research, or other third-party sources. The project methodology maturity models provide information whereby an organization can carry out a self-certification to grade its own processes from virtually nonexistent to the purist levels, principally as a means of identifying improvements and actions to take.

It is essential that the management of any organization identify and articulate its critical success factors (CSFs). These are the ground rules that determine the appropriateness of the environment in which the organization operates. The CSFs set out the culture, behavior, and actions for management to take to achieve its objectives relating to project methodologies. The guidance provided in the chapter should be easy to apply in practice.

➤ Assessing the Project Methodology Ecosystem

In the context of this book, a project management methodology is considered part of an overall larger ecosystem. The ecosystem can be viewed as a "give and take." Whenever you "touch" the ecosystem, there are things that are bound to occur. Table 2.1 lists what the ecosystem consists of.

Figure 2.2 shows the makeup of the project management methodology ecosystem. Remember that any sudden change to the core methodology will result in a change to many other areas, such as templates and a ripple effect on supportive

Table 2.1 Project management ecosystem components

Component	Example
Project standards and best practices	PMBOK, RUP, Java
Supportive processes	Change control
Project management infrastructure	PMO
Templates	Project brief
Performance metrics	ROI, BCA
Project activities	Testing
Project techniques	WBS, Use cases
Project tools	MS project
Project roles and responsibilities	Project teams
Core project methodology framework	PMLC process
Development methodologies toolset	Prince2, XP, Spiral

processes. Project managers wanting to deploy any methodology in an organization should realize this natural effect.

■ BEST PRACTICES FOR PROJECT METHODOLOGIES

Most projects share a common life cycle. This is not to say that these projects are all designed and executed the same way, but they remain universal, as they pass similar phases during the life cycle of the project. When dealing with any methodology, ask the following questions:

1. How do we ensure that our projects develop and deliver successful products? Is the methodology able to accurately capture requirements and effectively manage the project against those requirements?
2. How can we deploy projects more quickly, avoiding overruns and poor performance, and for better value, lower cost, and better functionality?

When looking at organizational project methodologies available today, we realize that certain methodologies work well and some do not. Some are more proactive than reactive. For those that are not well planned, the organizations will simply

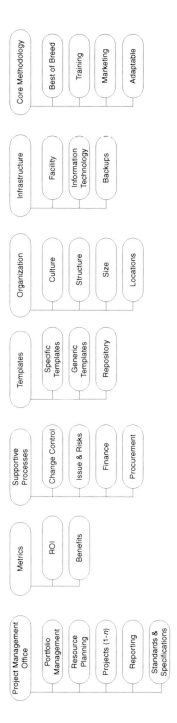

Figure 2.2 Project methodology ecosystem.

39

not have success with those methodologies. Competitors will overpower them and deliver products faster to the market, and the organization will face competitor lockout. Some of the following best practices are needed before designing, purchasing, or benchmarking a prospective solution:

➤ Provide standard proven processes and techniques.

➤ Benchmark or leverage the best that your industry has to offer.

➤ Create a list of "must-have" components.

➤ Recognize the necessary processes you need to complete projects.

➤ Consider the best cost and time schedules for your methodology.

➤ Determine what core competencies are important.

➤ Configure resources.

➤ Integrate with suppliers and parties.

➤ Understanding Project Life Cycles

After the project life cycle is defined, the project budget and technical aspects must be managed together. And this is important. Can you imagine delivering a project within cost and schedule but that the project does not meet its technical specifications? I think not—a project life cycle must be efficiently managed if the project is to be successful.

An *iteration* is defined as a distinct sequence of activities with an established plan and evaluation criteria resulting in an executable release. If we examine the set of illustrations describing the waterfall approach, we can see that an iterative approach does have advantages over a straightforward waterfall approach. This analogy should help reveal other ways to manage projects.

On many projects, where dates have been preset either by sales executives or senior corporate stakeholders, project managers often do not have the luxury of changing the fixed end date. Hence, how do you meet a fixed end date? Would a System Development Life Cycle (SDLC) or a Rapid Application

Development (RAD) approach work better for you (i.e., incremental versus an iterative approach)?

Delegates attending my project presentations often ask: "How do I make my view of the world work, when working with new technology projects?" "What methodology do I follow?" I always respond by stating that you have control over only the inputs you receive, and you define your projects based on those constraints. It's not up to you to start reorganizing the organization just for your project. First, see what's within your boundaries. Then act from there.

■ CIPOC—A CONCEPTUAL APPROACH

When I try to place any project life cycle or methodology into perspective, I always go back to the Client, Input, Process, Output, Clients (CIPOC) approach, a slight deviation from the "supplier" concept. It is one of the greatest examples of a primer that gives a high-level conceptual view of the way all project methodologies fit into the grand scheme of things (see Figure 2.3).

CIPOC works like this. A client has certain requirements for which he or she needs a certain solution. This can be a new skyscraper, submarine, spacecraft, software, or even a rock concert. It doesn't matter what kind of project. These client requirements are formed into inputs, which in turn serve as the

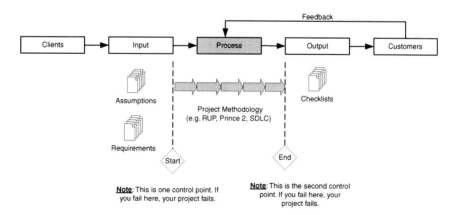

Figure 2.3 CIPOC technique to reflect methodology usage.

defining moments or starting point for the process—which can be virtually any methodology you want to use (e.g., Waterfall, SDLC, PACE, RUP, XP, MIL-STD-1612, PRINCE2). The project manager uses his or her chosen methodology and proceeds to design, build, test, and deploy the solution. These are the control points. When complete, an output has been generated that is then accepted by the client. The client can be involved anywhere in the CIPOC approach; the client readily provides feedback at any stage.

All assumptions must be made upfront at the onset of the project process start. This is one of the control points. If the project manager cannot control the assumptions, the project may come back and bite, irrespective of methodology employed.

If you need 500,000 kilowatts of power in a remote location, how do you do it? How do you meet your client's needs? You need an approach, and, typically, you would follow a CIPOC approach. Similarly, the Winter Olympics held in Salt Lake City was a phenomenal project itself. The Olympics organizers, too, would follow the CIPOC approach.

If we examine major companies such as Ernst & Young, RCG Information Technology, and IBM, we find that these major solutions companies have total "soup-to-nuts" project methodologies in place. These project methodologies embrace everything from the initial sales call, defining the solution, right through to deployment. They can identify the appropriate resources needed per project life-cycle phase (i.e., account executive, recruiter, designer, tester, project lead). These methodologies are well documented. If we examine other companies (e.g., home builders, software developers), we find that many don't have the luxury of such an elaborate project methodology in place. They simply adhere to projects in their own informal manner.

➤ Understanding Project Model Terminology

Project Feasibility and Justification

The project manager's first task is to become familiar with the feasibility of the project. He or she should reaffirm to his or her own satisfaction the findings of the original study, which may have been some time ago, certainly before he or she accepted the job. Thus, reaffirming the feasibility and justification of the project is crucial.

User Requirements

The most important phase in any project is to find out what is actually needed. Without proper establishment of the requirements, no one is certain what is really required. This is not covered fully in the Project Service Request (PSR); therefore, work and effort are needed at the start of the project. Subsequent time may be wasted if the user requirements are not established and understood.

System Design

After establishing and agreeing on the requirements, a high-level design of the main functions of the system can be produced. This is followed by considering the development of each of these main functions in more detail.

Detailed Design and Buy or Build

These follow the established meanings found in most development models. Each activity in the work breakdown structure (WBS) is given sufficient individual attention so that it is designed in detail ready for building. These phases apply equally to the design and creation of documentation as well as software. They also apply to hardware, except that items needed to run the software will be ordered from suppliers instead of building the items. The hardware design is determined by the software requirements.

Acceptance

The acceptance phase is the running of integration tests at system level to prove all documentation, software, hardware, and other equipment. These tests must be designed carefully and not left to the suppliers (of equipment, software, and documentation) to construct. Otherwise, we find that suppliers may test only the parts that work and may deliberately not consider the whole system, which may lead to problems for the end users. Notice that testing occurs throughout the project—not delayed until a single testing phase when and where it would be too late to rectify faults efficiently. This phase is about testing to accept the whole system, not testing to see if it works.

Commissioning

Every component is built, tested and integrated. *Commissioning* is the setting to work of the proven and integrated system. This is the time to introduce the end users to their relevant parts of the working system and then cut over to the live system. During this stage (or even before in some projects), user training takes place and the help desk is set up.

Completion and Post-Implementation Audit

When all stages are completed to the satisfaction and agreement of all parties, it is important that the project be recognized as complete. At this stage, it is crucial that the project manager document the following before starting another project:

➤ Job descriptions for operations staff.

➤ Job descriptions for systems staff.

➤ Working practices for operations and systems teams agreed on by management, operations manager, and systems manager.

➤ Rolling plan for update, upgrade, and replacement of equipment over the next two to five years.

➤ A plan to ensure that all documentation is complete and signed off.

➤ A plan to ensure that all contractors, subcontractors, and self are paid up-to-date.

➤ A postimplementation audit date for three to six months after project close-down.

In the postimplementation audit (PIA), the project manager returns a few months after responsibility for the new system has been assumed by the client (i.e., steady–state). The actual audit procedures should be determined initially, indicating that a team will return to see whether the system is working as designed. Most of this audit consists of ensuring that the project team is adhering to established working practices. It is quite surprising how people misinterpret documented procedures and invent ways around problems. These issues of documentation standards are beyond the scope of this book. The PIA has rarely been carried out in the past and is only now gaining a reputation for its usefulness.

➤ Roles and Responsibilities on a Project Life Cycle

Table 2.2 reveals typical roles and responsibilities that one would encounter on a project. The larger the project, the more roles and responsibilities would be added.

Table 2.2 Roles and responsibilities on the project life cycle

Roles	Responsibility
Verify resource allocation	Project Manager
Assign individual responsibilities	Project Manager
Verify project scope and change control	Project Manager
Estimate work packages and time to complete project	Project Manager
Monitor and control life cycles	Project Manager
Reduce uncertainty	Project Manager
Improve decision-making process	Sponsor
Attain effective solution	PM/Analysts
Establish continuous improvements to project	PM/QA
Maintain focus of project goals and objectives	Sponsor/PM
Provide continuous feedback to executives and stakeholders	Project Manager
Manage project plan	Project Manager
Avoid possible risks and issues	Project Manager
Maintain focus of schedules, budgets, and work plans	Sponsor

➤ Likes and Dislikes of Project Methodologies

Often, one person may give a project manager the best kudos and praise for adopting a certain project methodology, but too often, the kudos arise mainly from the ranks of the management layer. Methodologies are like an onion—just when you peel off one layer, you discover another layer waiting for you. Some of the pros and cons seen by managers and nonmanagers working on projects are listed in Table 2.3.

➤ Blueprints for Business Innovation

Because the introduction of a project management methodology and its processes possibly needs to be integrated into the existing business processes, it becomes necessary to stop to look at what we need to take care of before simply designing a methodology. Business process reengineering focuses on optimizing existing processes and facilitates the redesign of these processes if they are outdated and superfluous to departments or units, they do not meet clients' needs, or they are causing long delays for meeting organizational strategy.

Look at how Dell Computers is able to reconfigure its production lines for flexible, more rapid market demands. They

Table 2.3 What managers and nonmanagers think of methodologies

Project Managers Think	Nonmanagers (Team Members) Think
Methodologies define a set of deliverables.	Methodologies do not really represent what actually happens.
Methodologies adhere to a structured approach.	Phases are often overlapping with other phases.
Methodologies bring structure to a chaotic environment.	Methodologies are a waste of time and unnecessary overhead.
This is the way companies should be run.	No one clearly knows the true value of this path.
	Methodologies don't always reflect the technical requirements.

adapt more quickly than their competitors and apply great methodologies for their solutions. Look at how Walt Disney has moved beyond the realm of its theme parks by having its own line of cruise ships and entertainment—all innovative by design—reflecting that Disney is able to transcend the norm.

In Table 2.4, note that in any organization today, there are existing processes that directly interface with the aims and objectives of what many project managers are trying to do throughout the course of a project's life cycle. Remember that project management is about managing the triple constraints, which are (1) cost, (2) time, and (3) quality. It's not that simple for project or development managers to simply ignore existing processes to get their jobs done. The methodology should be tightly and seamlessly integrated into the existing processes, so much that they complement one another.

➤ Methodology Design

The focus of this section is how project methodologies can be developed to support projects in a company. Developing a project methodology and adapting it to the situation often deal with changes on many levels—changes in culture, processes,

Table 2.4 Examples of processes in organizations

Process	Function	Affects Project Management
Invoicing and posting of credits	Financial	✓
Purchasing of goods and services	Procurement	✓
Timesheet submission	Financial	✓
Financial monthly reporting	Financial	✓
Salaries	Financial	✓
Legal disputes and claims	Legal Council	✓
Recruitment of staff	Personnel	✓
Strategic prioritization of projects	Projects	✓
Quality control and assurance	QA	✓
Training	Training	✓
Profitability	Financial	✓

and information systems. A *culture* can provide project teams with a shared frame of reference and facilitate communication. The *processes* can provide a structure of activities in the projects, which helps new employees and can provide a common language. *Information systems* may be linked to the process and provide the tools that influence the daily work.

The research is based on active participation during the development of a methodology for product development. The case illustrates the tendency to focus on the process level and underestimate the importance of influencing the culture and adapting the current system to the new envisaged processes. The results are analyzed to provide increased understanding of the success factors when new project methodology is to be developed. The aim is to create a framework that can be used by companies that want to develop a project methodology or improve their existing project methodology.

With any new process, the way an organization works—and its entire culture—changes. Hence, it becomes crucial that the project manager not only develop the project management processes themselves but also create:

➤ Support plans.
➤ Communications plans.
➤ Deployment plans.

These elements facilitate cultural change in a company and are fundamental to a successful project management deployment. You should not "reinvent the wheel" for each client engagement. Tailor project management processes that best suit your needs. The project manager should understand business processes and be able to merge them with current and tested best practices to quickly and effectively produce a tailored, client-specific set of project processes. It's not easy— developing processes is a science in itself. The question is: Do you have time to implement these processes on your own? Or, is your time running out? How much help is needed to design these processes to support your project framework?

■ PROJECT METHODOLOGIES DEMYSTIFIED

We now examine the relationship between methodology size, project size, and problem size. This discussion can be tricky because there is a tendency to think that more people must solve larger problems.

Project size and methodology are connected by a positive feedback loop. With relatively few people, relatively little methodology is needed. With less "weight," they work more productively. With greater productivity, they can address a larger problem with their smaller team and lighter methodology. On the other hand, when more people are assigned to a project, they need more coordination (i.e., more methodology). The heavier methodology lowers their productivity; therefore, more people are needed to accomplish the same work. Methodology grows more slowly than project size, so eventually they get to a point where they can solve the problem and manage the coordination activities (assuming sensible management).

Therefore, for a given problem, you need fewer people if you use a lighter methodology and more people if you use a heavier methodology. However, there is a limit to the size of problem that can be solved with a given number of people, and that limit is higher for a large team using a heavier methodology than for a small team using a lighter methodology (i.e., at some point, you will need both a large team and a heavier methodology). The difficulty is that there is no reliable way to determine the problem size at the start of a project and no way to know the minimum number of people needed to solve it. The number of people varies with the people in question. Finally, as the project grows in size, a different combination of methodology and project size becomes optimal.

To begin to consider what constitutes a good and effective project management or development methodology, you need to clearly understand what phases are available to use, within all the project and development methodologies that face you as a project manager. The most common phases you would likely encounter when discussing or designing a methodology are discussed in the following sections.

➤ Discovery/Concept/Idea

A well-conceived idea is the creative stuff that makes every-thing important. It's why the project started in the first place. There is no launch if there is no acceptable initial idea. Brain-storming is an effective technique to help you develop a prime idea. Be aware of the effect that the external environment (cus-tomers, competitors, market, etc.) has on the idea. In the con-cept stage, the exact definition of the idea and strategy is derived. The objective is to develop a protocol with defined tar-get markets, product concepts, and attributes.

➤ Engagement/Concept

Because each project is unique and must be approached very differently from the next because of client requirements and demands, in the engagement or concept phase, the project manager and sales executive actually meet with the client and discuss possibilities and begin to extend the communications process between the parties involved. This is often the most important phase as it sets the standard going forward. This can initially be a single occurrence or a series of meetings that brings the stakeholders together. It identifies key role players in the project and starts setting responsibilities.

➤ Analysis/Feasibility

The analysis or feasibility phase determines that the project has been thoroughly assessed and deemed economically or strategically feasible to continue. If the analysis weighs against the project's success, the project is discontinued or returned to executives for further discussions. It is highly recommended that projects be analyzed before commencing to the next phase of the project life cycle or methodology.

➤ Strategy Planning

Every company needs to have a system for deciding on and for-mulating the necessity and priority of launching any project or product. Whether a new design or new release of software, the strategists need to plan within the framework of the business model. The strategy planning would allow decisions about launching additional projects to support a priority project or delaying certain projects to favor a more important project's getting to market.

➤ Feasibility Assessment

Before committing time and resources to any development, it may be necessary to establish the *need* for the project. Sometimes, it's not feasible to commit the organization to even attempt the project because it simply duplicates another effort or costs too much to gain a successful foothold in the marketplace. Additionally, the technical feasibility of the project may be unknown, and without performing a proper feasibility study of the technology, the project would result in negative cost and schedule delays.

➤ System Analysis

After the project is launched, it becomes vitally important to establish client requirements to start designing the eventual system or product. At this stage, the project team should use techniques to fully understand what the project should deliver.

➤ Design/Development

On any project methodology, one of the key phases is the design or development phase. The phase represents the solution build. Key staff—such as designers, architects, or engineers—develop a solution based on either partial or full user requirements. This design will form the basic building blocks from which the project team will work.

➤ Deployment/Execution

After the project has been built, tested, and proven to work as designed and specified, the project is ready for installation or rollout. It is during this phase that the product or system is finally assembled and installed. In addition to simply implementing a system, users must be trained.

➤ Testing

This phase indicates the formal testing of the solution. Testing can be done either incrementally or at the end of a development phase if following a waterfall approach.

➤ Quality Assurance

In the quality assurance phase, the solution is validated and tested against the initial specifications of the project.

➤ Training/Education

Before any system or project is fully deployed, users need to be identified and trained. This phase may involve establishing the training requirements for the project and generating either the necessary training courses or documentation.

➤ Rollout/Implementation/Deployment

This phase is the delivery of the solution within the client organization. The rollout takes effect when the system is ready to be installed either in a series of small increments or as a full-blown deployment. During this phase, it is crucial to have an implementation plan and schedule to assist with the details of rolling out the project to the client.

➤ Maintenance/Support/Operations

After the project has been finalized and the product launched, it is considered operational or in production. Therefore, the product must now be maintained. Many products need constant updates or changes. For example, after a new software is launched, it is likely that some updates will be needed. Therefore, the project needs to address exactly how postproject changes will be handled and executed. Considerations such as how incremental changes will be implemented must be resolved. On many other projects, fulfillment and restocking of vital spare parts—including the vendors' support—are crucial in making this project a success. (Methodology support is discussed in Chapter 6.) In this phase, the organization or client introduces operational support for the project once completed. Tasks such as arranging help desk support, service level agreements, and monitoring and diagnostics are performed in this phase.

■ THE IMPORTANCE OF IT METHODOLOGIES

As many industries use information technology and focus on the development of software, it is appropriate to describe the IT environment to explain why different methodologies are needed for different things. For example, many construction companies that use the standard waterfall methodology are today using IT methodologies—such as RAD—to bring in their predictive and "heavy" schedules more quickly than before. And it appears to be working successfully.

With almost all IT projects today, we typically encounter any one of the following scenarios in which we need to adopt a development methodology. An IT project may consist of three core tiers:

1. Graphics User Interface tier (front-end). Usually done by visual development languages using tools such as Visual Studio.NET, Java.

2. Application middle tier. Usually addressed by a business-centric methodology.

3. Database tier (back-end). Usually accessing one or many databases to retrieve data or information, using tools such as SQL, Java, or object components.

The same development cannot be used for each tier. For example, you are tasked with an IT project in which you have to use only the top layer—the front-end—then you need to consider your specific development options. They may be application specific. The same applies for the other two tiers.

■ IDENTIFYING YOUR PROJECT MATURITY

Many companies are very aware of the important role project management plays in their companies, but many are somehow unable or unwilling to make a transition to develop their project philosophy to the next level. Companies want to know exactly (1) how well they are currently doing and (2) where they would like to be on a project maturity level. After all, a company is more than just existing processes, policy, and procedures.

To use an analogy, if you had to take a life-saving drug that was developed by a company certified at capability maturity model (CMM) Level 5, compared to a company with only a CMM Level 1 certification, you would go with the company with the Level 5 certification. After all, it gives you the sense of a mature project-based organization, which has its act together. If project management is to take a leading role in a company, it needs to be good in a few areas, which follow:

➤ A project management philosophy is firmly entrenched in the company.
➤ Management has bought into project management as a core competency.
➤ The company is focused on making projects succeed.
➤ The necessary project processes and infrastructure are established.
➤ An effective reporting system is established.
➤ The project methodology and development methodologies are well documented.
➤ Project staff is provided continuous training to update their skills.
➤ Project information is communicated continuously.

➤ Projects are monitored against performance.

➤ Quality and delivery excellence are built into all projects from day one.

➤ Projects are routinely audited for compliance with company standards.

➤ The Capability Maturity Model (CMM)

So what is the buzz all about when it comes to CMM and why should we care? The Software Engineering Institute's (SEI) CMM is not actually a life cycle methodology, but rather sets of strategies for improving the software process on a projects. Therefore, I have not included CMM in Chapter 3. Many companies using CMM are stuck in a default waterfall methodology mentality and have neglected the spiral or iterative development methodologies. This is not CMM's fault at all, but project managers should understand that the waterfall approach is not always the best way to proceed. However, CMM has made advances in covering aspects of iterative methodology projects, although this doesn't always come across as being communicated to the project community. CMM tends to overemphasize inspections, peer reviews, and enforces strict quality assurance (QA) adherence, forcing many projects into paper and meeting "overload," which is also not good.

The primary objective for any company is to achieve a Level 3 CMM certification. Many companies are rated on how well their processes and systems meet the best project standards. In other words, if it does the prescribed set of foundation project activities, it is a Level 2. If it then does a prescribed set of project activities as a "company," it is Level 3, and so on. Essentially designed by SEI to help organizations overcome their problems, the system provides an effective and proven method for gradually gaining control of and improving product development processes, a yardstick against which companies periodically measure their production process, and data with which to prioritize and manage improvement efforts. I have included CMM in this book because many people are convinced that it is a variant of a project methodology, which is untrue. The areas of CMM are: (1) SW-CMM for software, (2) SE-CMM for systems engineering, (3) IPD-CMM for integrated product development, (4) SA for software acquisition, and (5) P-CMM for human resources.

An instrument for assessing a company's current maturity level and project practices is a software capability evaluation (SCE), which determines whether a company "says what it does and does what it says." Therefore, to gauge a company's actual performance, you need to perform an accurate assessment, which is not always done; instead, CMM is applied as both the development and assessment standard. The RUP or ISO 12207 standards are other references.

Together, this set of strategies is being integrated into what is now known as CMM Integration (CMMI). The CMMI is a more activity-based approach, which integrates many of industry's modern best practices and discourages an alignment with the waterfall mentality. Hence, CMMI is more iterative in concept versus the traditional CMM waterfall concept.

CMM describes both unique product development practices and the common management practices that any organization must perform. These practices are organized into five levels, each level describing increasing control and management of the production environment, starting with ad-hoc performance and culminating in controlled, structured, continuous improvement. An evaluation of the organization's practices against the model, called an *assessment,* determines the level, establishing where the organization stands and which management practices the organization should focus on to see the highest return on investment.

SEI Fellow Watts S. Humphrey created CMM in 1987. CMM is more than 10 years old and has greatly influenced the software industry by having us focus on the development and project process. However, technological shifts are taking place that require development to be more proactive. Originally funded by the U.S. Department of Defense, CMM is used by more than 5,000 government and private companies in more than 42 countries. Large portions of the Level 5 assessments that have been made are based in India. One of its primary goals is to identify and reduce errors during the initial coding process and thereby reduce the amount of rework required from finding errors during testing. The CMM is organized into five maturity levels:

➤ *Level 1: Initial.* This describes a company with an immature or undefined process. The software process is characterized as ad hoc and, occasionally, even chaotic or unpredictable. Few processes are defined, and success depends on individual effort and heroics.

➤ *Level 2: Repeatable.* Project management structures and controls begin here. Basic project management processes are established to track cost, schedule, and functionality. The necessary process discipline is in place to repeat earlier successes on projects with similar applications. The key components of project management at this level are: requirements management, software project planning, software project tracking and oversight, software subcontract management, software quality assurance, and software configuration management.

➤ *Level 3: Defined.* The software process for both management and engineering activities is documented, standardized, and integrated into a standard software process for the organization. All projects use an approved, tailored version of the organization's standard software process for developing and maintaining software. The key process areas at Level 3 address both project and organizational issues. At this level, the company establishes an infrastructure to institutionalize software engineering and management processes across all projects. Compliance with these standards for all projects and by all project managers and development teams is needed.

➤ *Level 4: Managed.* Detailed measures of the software process and product quality are collected. Both the software process and products are quantitatively understood, controlled, and evaluated by an executive and related staff. The key process areas at Level 4 focus on establishing a quantitative understanding of both the software process and the software work products being built. They are quantitative process management and software quality management. It is at this level that analysis tools such as function point analysis and other performance metrics are implemented.

➤ *Level 5: Optimized.* Continuous process improvement is enabled by quantitative feedback from the process and from piloting innovative ideas and technologies. The key process areas at Level 5 cover the issues that both the organization and the projects must address to implement continual, measurable software process improvement—defect prevention, technology change management, and process change management.

Getting your company to make an effort to move up the CMM ladder may not be easy. CMM focuses mainly on activities and supporting documents associated with a conventional waterfall process, such as plans, specifications, QA audits, inspections, and formal documented processes and procedures. It's very documentation orientated, and this drive to produce more documents can actually slow a company down. However, this needs to be better addressed by CMM.

Many companies simply do not have the commitment, time, and resources to graduate beyond Level 1 or 2 on the CMM scale. So they stay there. The downside is that these companies eventually lose business, because nobody wants to hire a company who is rated as "ad-hoc" Level 1 on the CMM scale. There are even fewer companies identified at Levels 4 or 5. However, at these levels, you will undoubtedly find that more reviews, inspections, and meetings take place just to satisfy the CMM auditing and certification requirements.

In conclusion, assessing your project management in your company and thereby gauging yourself against others requires that you apply some form of metrics to your projects. CMM/CMMI techniques are a way to do this, showing you know how your project management measures up to the rest of the industry. It's a clear way to determine if "you're doing what you say you can do."

■ USING THE MIND-MAPPING CONCEPT

The one effective way to lay out the envisaged framework of a project methodology is to illustrate or mind map it on paper first, thereby addressing all areas of the organization. Figure 2.4 shows a typical mind-map framework. You can easily start developing a framework in this manner. Look at the way we mentally organize our thoughts—as this is very relevant to thinking about methodologies. If you cannot map out a process, it is futile. However, the human brain is so sophisticated that the mind-mapping method guides the methodology development process. Your brain initially encounters biochemical or electromagnetic resistance along its pathway, where thoughts are reduced. It's like trying to clear a path through a forest. The first time is a struggle, as you have to fight your way through the undergrowth. The second time you travel that way, it is easier because of the clearing you made on the first pass. Frequent repetitive events make it easier for you. Likewise, creating mind maps and documenting them in creative graphical formats assist the human brain in receiving, holding, analyzing output, and control. What happens in your brain when you want to design a project methodology? The answer is both simple and amazingly complex. Every thought or bit of information entering the brain—experiences and memory (template, code, word) can be represented as a central sphere that radiates tens, hundreds, thousands, millions of hooks—which represent associations—that in turn have their own links and connections. The number of associations you have can be thought of as your memory or database. As you read these words, you can be assured that in your brain is an analytical super computer that is far superior to many of the world's most advanced computers. The mind-mapping technique offers us the following approach:

➤ It has a central theme.
➤ It has branches of themes, which radiate from this central core.
➤ These branches contain keywords and are connected.

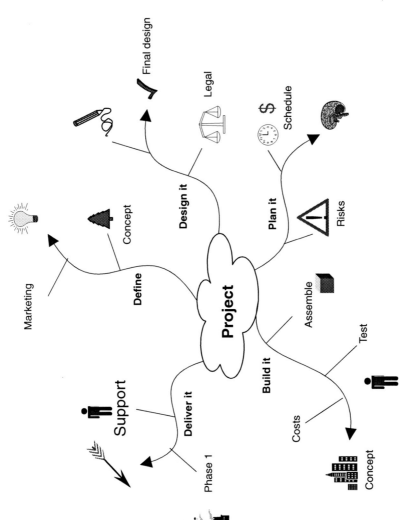

Figure 2.4 Mind-mapping methodology.

Table 2.5 Reference points

Association	URL
Association for Project Management	www.apm.org.uk
Malcolm Baldrige Model	www.quality.nist.gov
BS 5750 (British Standards Institute)	www.bsi.org.uk
EFQM (European Foundation for Quality Management)	www.efqm.org
ISO 9002 (International Standards Institute)	www.iso.ch
ITIL (Information Technology Infrastructure Library)	www.ccta.gov.uk/itil
PMBOK (Project Management Institute)	www.pmi.org
PRINCE (Projects in Controlled Environments)	www.ccta.gov.uk/prince
SSADM (Structured Systems Analysis and Design Method)	www.ccta.gov.uk/bestpractice/ssadm

➤ This together creates a "picture" of the solution or idea you need.

A mind-mapping method can be extended easily to designing or conceptualizing any project methodology in existence in a graphical manner. From this, anything is possible.

■ REFERENCES TO VARIOUS METHODOLOGIES

For additional information on project management methodology, see Table 2.5.

■ SUMMARY

In this chapter, we see that a generic project methodology contains at least nine basic elements: roles, skills, activities, techniques, tools, teams, deliverables, standards, and quality measures. Different methodologies are, however, needed depending on the project size (number of people being coordinated), the criticality of the systems being created, and the priorities of the project. This all counts when deciding on the correct methodology to use. Any comparison of methodologies should include these dimensions, and their relationship to the needs of the project or organization should be assessed.

■ QUESTIONS

1. Define the term *project life cycle.*

2. Methodologies are the best weapon in a company's arsenal if they want to avoid what?

3. List five reasons that projects fail and state what possible solutions could prevent failure.

4. What does the term *project strategy* mean? Is it the same as a *business strategy?*

5. What are the five levels of the capability maturity model?

6. List three reasons why team members would dislike methodologies?

Chapter 3

Project Management Frameworks

Sometimes you are faced with a project that could cost a small fortune—from hundreds of thousands of dollars to a few million dollars. As project manager, you are charged with delivering the project within cost, specification, and schedule. This is often the opening line for many project managers today. Without an effective project framework in place, it will not matter what you do—projects will undoubtedly be more complicated and troublesome. In this chapter, I provide a few project methodologies or frameworks used today across industry, as well as the components that make up these project methodologies. Sometimes, one methodology framework is not the most appropriate to use—you may need to adapt to some other methodology.

Vinod Khosla (April 2001) in "GigaTrends," *Wired* magazine, states: "Most of our predictions are based on very linear thinking. That's why they will most likely be wrong!"

In fact, the very success of the company could depend on the successful outcome of projects, so it becomes essential that you minimize as much risk as possible and approach projects in such a way that it almost guarantees success. But how do we do this? One technique uses a tried and tested project methodology, which covers all possible areas when a project starts. By employing the appropriate methodology, project managers are likely to deliver the solutions their clients want. I introduce and clarify two types of methodologies. Although they go hand-in-hand, there is a difference.

➤ Project management methodologies (this lays the high-level project framework).

➤ Development methodologies (this provides the detail on system design and development).

It is likely that you will encounter a project that consists of both a project methodology and a development methodology. You have the shell—dealing with the project approach, competencies, and so on—and then the content of the shell—which deals with the specific development approach. You can see more about development methodologies in Chapter 4 of this book. We concentrate on purely project methodologies in this chapter.

Some people would like to challenge my contention that many project managers often live a lie, perhaps by force, when it comes to adhering to a methodology. This normally happens when a project manager is assigned a project already half completed; he or she simply follows his or her best guess and proceeds from there—often ignoring key issues and steps that make a truly great project. He or she continues to plan, predict, and deliver as best as possible, working the best way he or she knows. It appears that many project managers do not want to create the wrong perception on their projects. As soon as the project starts, project managers jump in, build the solution one way, and when they encounter trouble, pretend to build it another way, flying by the seat of their pants. The lesson here is that rigid methodologies are often far too constraining and fall short in delivering a project into production. When we review many projects that have failed, we see that overhead is often created to prove that the methodology is on track.

When starting a project, many project managers gather as much documentation pertaining to the project as they can. They start creating elaborate project Gantt schedules, using sophisticated software tools, extending it to Pert charts, critical path networks, believing that by following a few simple techniques and a trick here and there, the project will start

Methodology /Life Cycle	Risk	Ease to Implement	Resource Intensive	Frequent Changes	Easy to Manage	Scope Creep	Reliability	Document Oriented	Project Approach
Waterfall	Low	Easy	 (icon)	✗	✓	✓	✓	✓	Phased
SDLC	Med	Average	(icon)	✓	✓	✓	✓	✓	Phased
PACE	Low	Easy	(icon)	✗	✓	✓	✓	✓	Phased
RUP	Med	Difficult	(icon)	✓	✗	✓	✓	✓	Phased
New Product Development	Med	Average	 (icon)	✓	✗	✓	✓	✓	Phased
PMI Life Cycle	Med	Easy	 (icon)	✓	✓	✓	✓	✓	Phased
PRINCE2	Med	Easy	 (icon)	✗	✓	✓	✓	✓	Phased
DOD-STD-2167	Med	Average	 (icon)	✓	✗	✓	✓	✓	Phased

Figure 3.1   Assessing project management frameworks.

65

magically taking shape. However, being smart in a few project techniques and being flashy are not synonymous with great results. What's forgotten here is adhering to the methodology, as well as to the development model. You don't have to rigidly follow the project process step-by-step; you can tailor the framework at any stage for each project or solution.

Figure 3.1 shows a typical flow of common problems identified on a project, the causes of the problems, and the solution. Look at the problem "over schedule." We see that it is caused by the waterfall methodology being used (e.g., takes too long). The solution is to use an iterative approach, as discussed in more detail in Chapter 4.

■ SELECTING YOUR METHODOLOGY

Every company currently without a project management framework needs to identify, select, tailor, or build one before managing a project. Some structure is necessary. If management wants their company to be successful in a project-based world, they should start moving. They should think about the following objectives before deciding on a project management methodology:

➤ The overall company strategy—how competitive are we as a company?

➤ The size of the project team and/or scope to be managed.

➤ The priority of the project.

➤ How critical the project is to the company.

➤ How flexible the methodology and its components are.

➤ Best Project Methodology Practices

To ensure a project's success throughout the entire methodology, project managers and project office managers should adhere to the following recommended best practices when selecting, building, or tailoring a project management methodology:

➤ Use standard-proven processes and techniques.

➤ Draw on best industry practices and trends.

➤ Use best practices to reduce common pitfalls.

➤ Look at implementation time and cost reduction.

➤ Minimize excess templates and administration.

➤ Consult industry leaders and subject matter experts (SMEs).

➤ Acknowledge the best path for project implementation.

➤ Recognize what should and should not be implemented.

The following summarizes four key principles in methodology design that should be reinforced:

1. Use larger methodologies for larger teams.
2. Use denser methodologies for more critical projects.
3. Weight is costly.
4. Interactive, face-to-face communication is most effective.

■ METHODOLOGY UTILIZATION

When using any project framework methodology, ensure that it doesn't become bureaucratic and so administrative in detail that it actually stifles any sense of creativity or overrides common sense. For example, you have a project that must be completed within four months. You have to design and deploy a new product. As project manager, you understand that you cannot spend all your time creating elaborate documentation and hold meetings to create new processes. Time is against you; therefore, it would be wise to first adopt the correct methodology. Developing the organization's project management framework is one of the core foundations of any business to ensure project success. This framework should include:

➤ A total project management approach from start to finish.

➤ The key phases that the company would possibly use.

➤ Inclusion of quality gates or checkpoints during each phase.

➤ Necessary review points between each phase.

➤ Preproject and postproject phases (e.g., sales, operations).

➤ Project templates.

➤ Project processes per phase (i.e., change control, risk).

Using a proven project framework based on industry best practices and *tailoring* that approach to fit your organization's culture and practices are the keys to success. In the following section of this chapter, we review different types of methodology frameworks used by industry today.

■ RATIONAL UNIFIED PROCESS (RUP) PROJECT FRAMEWORK

The Rational Unified Process, or more affectionately referred to as *RUP,* is a customizable project methodology framework aimed primarily at software development. It is a complete software development process framework that comes with several out-of-the-box examples. Processes derived from RUP vary from lightweight—which address the needs of small projects—to

Table 3.1 The components of the RUP framework

4 phases
8 iterations (minimum)
9 workflows
57 activities
270 activity steps (approximately)
114 artifacts
38 roles (up to 38 people)

more complex heavyweight projects. To date, projects of all sizes have successfully used RUP.

This methodology enhances team productivity and delivers software best practices to the project team through a set of components, which in turn consist of guidelines, templates, and best practices from thousands of development projects. From large-scale enterprise to agile projects, RUP allows organizations to develop projects more rapidly and deliver quality even when using this process. Table 3.1 and Figure 3.2 show key areas that make up RUP.

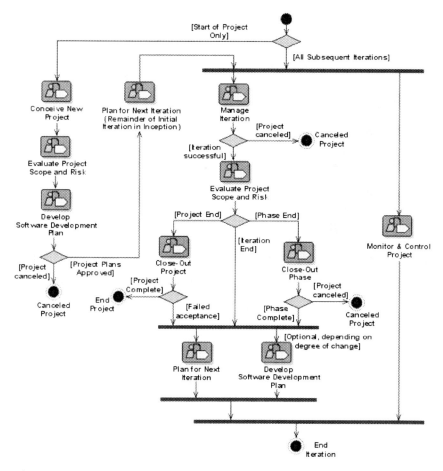

Figure 3.2 RUP project management process. *Source:* Life Cycles of the Rational Unified Process. Reprinted with permission.

RUP is not merely a process. It is valuable because it embodies many of the best project management practices available today, thereby making it a flexible framework to which project managers can apply their solutions. In other words, you could consider RUP to be a road map for project managers, analysts, testers, and so on. This allows resources to use a common project management terminology and a component "kit" on how to manage projects. If you already know project management, RUP merely becomes a checklist. However, if you are new to project management, RUP gives you a nice overview. Companies such as Wells Fargo and Merrill Lynch and numerous others have used RUP successfully (see Figure 3.3).

The preferred approach to using RUP is to first determine what is missing from the organization's project management environment. After this assessment has been completed, decide how much change the organization can handle. For example, if a company's biggest problem is requirements gathering, RUP offers this process. When this company starts using RUP, you can reassess how successful their requirements-gathering process has worked. Over time, a RUP-based project goes through

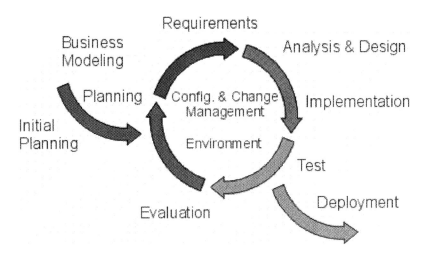

Figure 3.3 RUP cycle. *Source:* Life Cycles of the Rational Unified Process. Reprinted with permission.

four distinct phases: inception, elaboration, construction, and transition. Each phase contains one or more iterations. In each iteration, efforts are expended in various amounts to each of several disciplines (or workflows) such as requirements, analysis and design, testing, and configuration management. The key advantage of RUP is reduction of risks (see Figure 3.4).

Virtually any company can use and customize RUP to suit the needs of its projects. This implies that RUP is as heavy or light as the project wants to go. The implementation of RUP could take from a few weeks to a few years, depending on how much process is required. Above all, use common sense when implementing RUP, as no major tools and techniques are needed. In the future, many companies will use RUP as a project management framework, whereby they can "hang" their best practices. RUP also provides information to help in using other Rational tools for better software development, but does

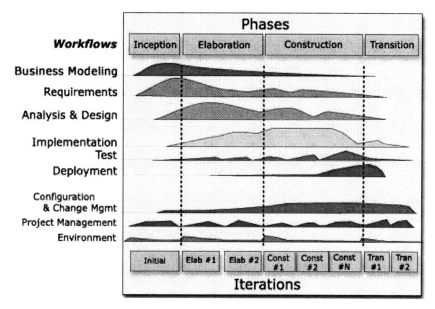

Figure 3.4 RUP life-cycle phases comparison. *Source:* Life Cycles of the Rational Unified Process. Reprinted with permission.

not require the Rational toolset for effective application to an organization. It, therefore, allows you to tailor the process if none of the "out-of-the-box" road maps suit your organization or project. RUP emphasizes the adoption of certain best practices of modern software development as a way to reduce the risk inherent in developing new software. These best practices are:

➤ Develop iteratively.
➤ Manage requirements.
➤ Use component-based architectures.
➤ Model visually.
➤ Continuously verify quality.
➤ Control change.

■ PRINCE2 PROJECT FRAMEWORK

PRINCE2 is an acronym for Projects in Controlled Environments (second version) and is now the United Kingdom's de facto standard for IT project management. The Central Computing and Telecommunications Agency (CCTA) originally developed this structured project management methodology, which now forms part of the Office of Government Commerce (OCG)—a government agency—for the development and implementation of IT projects. In fact, this methodology is now so popular that many companies hire only PRINCE2-certified project managers. More and more companies are moving toward adopting this as their standard project approach. Companies such as British Rail, Nat West, Hitachi, BT, London Underground, and Royal Mail, among many others, benefit from using PRINCE2. Some of the many features of this methodology are:

➤ A defined project management structure.
➤ Flexible decision-making points.
➤ A system of plans for resources and technical issues.
➤ A set of control procedures.

➤ A focus on products—deliverables to the client.

➤ A focus on project deliverables throughout the project.

This methodology can readily be applied to non-IT projects as well; therefore, even the construction industry can use this methodology. It is a project management methodology specifically designed to be generic and independent of any particular project type and complexity. This makes PRINCE2 methodology even more interesting to consider. It is nonproprietary, easy to use, and, with some basic training, an excellent approach. Similar to the Dynamic Systems Development Methodology (DSDM) described in Chapter 4, its use is dramatically on the increase in both the public and private sectors. A feature in PRINCE2 not seen in other methodologies is the concept of *assuring progress* from three separate but linked perspectives. Most organizations that adopt PRINCE2 choose it primarily for its wide applicability and use the pieces that actually "work for them."

Figure 3.5 shows that PRINCE2 is a process-orientated approach for project management. Each process has its inputs and outputs with associated project tasks and activities to be carried out. The methodology shows us that a project is decomposed in manageable phases, allowing efficient command and control. For example, look at *project planning*. This phase is mainly interested in focusing on results rather than planning when the activities will be done. PRINCE2 is largely driven by its business case (see templates), which describes the business justification, rationale, and motivation for the project. The same applies to all phases shown in the figure. Integrating this methodology into a company's existing culture and processes may require the insight and assessment by certified PRINCE2 project managers, who are knowledgeable of this methodology.

On the upper tier of the illustration, note that the project(s) may report to a corporate program management function. Start at "Directing a Project," which runs from the start-up of the project until the close. This process is aimed at the project board, who manages by exception, monitors via reports, and controls through a number of decision points.

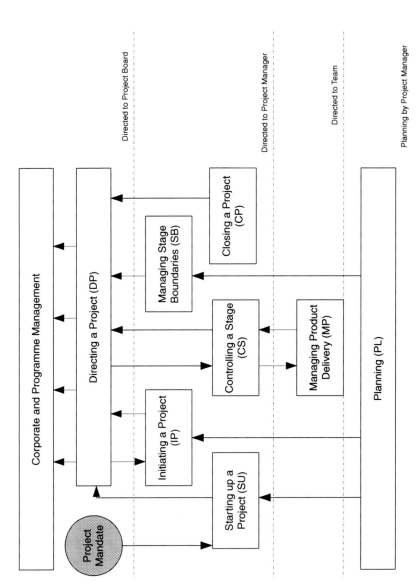

Figure 3.5 PRINCE2 life cycle.

➤ PRINCE2 Phases

The key processes of the project board are these four main areas:

1. Initiating (starting the project on the right foot).
2. Stage boundaries (commitment of more resources after checking results reached).
3. Ad hoc direction (monitoring progress, providing advice and guidance, and reacting to exception situations).
4. Project closure (confirming the project outcome and controlled close).

This process does not cover the day-to-day activities of the project manager. In the middle tier, we find the phases, which are equally important to any project manager wishing to adhere to this methodology. The phases are:

➤ *Starting up a project.* The first process in PRINCE2 is a preproject process, designed to ensure that the prerequisites for initiating the project are in place. The process expects the existence of a project mandate, which defines in high-level terms the reason for the project and what outcome is sought. Start-up of a project should be very short and should include the following:

— Ensuring that the information required for the project team is available.

— Designing and appointing the project team.

— Creating the initiation stage plan.

— Agreeing whether there is sufficient justification to proceed with the project.

— Establishing a stable management basis on which to proceed.

— Documenting and confirming that an acceptable business case exists for the project.

— Ensuring a form and accepted foundation to the project before starting work.

- —Agreeing to the commitment of resources for the first phase of the project.
- —Providing the baseline for the decision-making processes required during the project's life.
- —Ensuring that the investment of time and effort required by the project is made wisely, taking in account the risks to the project.

➤ *Managing stage boundaries.* This process provides the project board with key decision points on whether to continue with the project. The objectives of this process are to:

- —Assure the project board that all deliverables planned in the current stage have been completed as defined.
- —Provide the information needed for the project board to assess the continuing viability of the project.
- —Provide the project board with information needed to approve the current phase's completion and authorize the start of the next phase.
- —Record any measurements or lessons that can help later phases of the project(s).

➤ *Controlling a stage.* This process describes the monitoring and control activities of the project manager involved in ensuring that a phase stays on course and reacts to unexpected events. The process forms the core of the project manager's effort on the project and handles the day-to-day project management tasks and activities. Throughout each phase, there is a cycle consisting of:

- —Authorizing work to be done.
- —Gathering progress status on work.
- —Watching for changes.
- —Reviewing the situation.
- —Reporting.
- —Implementing the necessary corrective action.

➤ *Managing product delivery.* The aim of this process is to ensure that planned products are created and delivered, by:

—Making sure that work on products allocated to the team is effectively authorized and agreed on.

—Ensuring that the work conforms to the requirements of interfaces identified in the work package.

—Ensuring the work is done.

—Assessing work progress and forecasts regularly.

—Obtaining approval for the completed products.

➤ *Closing a project.* The aim of this process is to execute a controlled close to the project. The process covers the project manager's work to wrap up the project either at its end or at premature closure. Most of the work is to prepare the input for the project board so that they may sign off the project. The objectives for this phase are:

—Checking the extent to which the objectives set out in the project initiation document have been met.

—Confirming the extent of the fulfillment of the project initiation document and the client's satisfaction with the deliverables.

—Obtaining formal acceptance of the deliverables.

—Ensuring to what extent all expected products have been handed over and accepted by the client.

—Confirming that maintenance and operation arrangements are in place (where appropriate).

—Making any recommendations for follow-up actions.

—Capturing the lessons learned from the project and completing a lessons learned document.

—Preparing the end project report.

—Notifying the host organization of the intent to disband the project resources.

On the lowest tier, we find the planning process. It is important because it considers key project processes, which are:

➤ Planning an initiation phase.
➤ Planning a project.

➤ Planning a phase.

➤ Producing an exception plan.

Overall, PRINCE2 proves to be a sensible and practical project methodology. The best feature is that no license is required for using this methodology, except one obtaining the required documentation. Additionally, it is not necessary to purchase special project management tools, as PRINCE2 allows use of any project management tool to manage projects. Project managers who are familiar with PRINCE2 are able to:

➤ Establish terms of reference as a prerequisite to the start of the project.

➤ Use a defined structure for delegation, authority, and communication.

➤ Divide the project into manageable stages for more accurate planning.

➤ Ensure resource commitment from management is part of any approval to proceed.

➤ Provide regular but brief management reports.

➤ Keep meetings with management and stakeholders to a minimum but schedule them at vital points in the project.

➤ Required PRINCE2 Artifacts

There are essential artifacts required by a typical PRINCE2 project. First, the business case artifact used by PRINCE2 is a reasoning or justification of the project. After all, as mentioned in Chapter 1, companies must focus on pursuing only those key strategic projects that produce innovative products and services. Together with this, project managers must ensure that all project risks be identified in the business case.

The business case should be routinely updated to reflect any change to the project, should new risks be identified. It is true that much time is spent on the business case, but this ensures proper planning and coordination. Therefore, the business case gives a clear picture of what is to be delivered. At the start of a project, the product specification is drawn up, which reduces the risk of delivering the wrong product. Although the PRINCE2 methodology does not directly deal with social or "soft" management skills, such as negotiations, presentation techniques, coaching, or leadership, it is necessary for a project manager to possess these skills to be successful.

If your company plans to implement PRINCE2, you would most likely start by training your key staff on the best practices and detail on the methodology and then provide overview training to those who would need to be aware of the methodology. Advantages and disadvantages of using PRINCE2 are discussed in the following sections.

➤ Advantages of PRINCE2

- ➤ The method is independent of the application domain such as IT software development, marketing, building and construction, and change management. Domain-specific methods such as DSDM, product development methods, or domain-specific standards can be applied in the PRINCE2 teams. This way, the method is generically applicable to any project. PRINCE2 provides a layer over the disciplines that are needed in the project because it defines a flexible "project language" that suits multidiscipline project teams. Therefore, the method bridges the gap between IT and business, for instance.

- ➤ The method is in the public domain, and services (training, consultancy, and tools) can be obtained from several independent suppliers.

- ➤ The method has active user groups in the United Kingdom and the Netherlands.

- ➤ The method is applicable to small and large mega-projects.

- ➤ The method focuses on project results in terms of the standard time, cost, quality, and functionality parameters but also has a strong focus on business case and the benefits the project results deliver.

➤ The method integrates change management that controls the changing environment.

➤ The method uses management by objectives and management by exception approaches.

➤ **Disadvantages of PRINCE2**

➤ It is a method and not a cure for any project. People who use PRINCE2 should continue to think.

➤ Some people apply and interpret the methodology in a rigid way and do not tailor it to the project at hand. Huge bureaucracies might be constructed if all checklists are used in a paper format and not adapted to the project.

➤ Human factor or soft issues are not within the scope of the methodology and are desperately needed for project success.

■ SYSTEM DEVELOPMENT LIFE CYCLE (SDLC) METHODOLOGY

Many projects follow the classic waterfall approach, and it is fairly straightforward to conceptualize. No rocket science is needed here. You simply have to focus on the logical progression of what needs to happen on the project. The SDLC is in essence a waterfall methodology. Successful companies such as Johnson & Johnson, Novartis, Adventis, American Express, and Nokia use and adhere to an SDLC approach. Table 3.2 describes the basic methodology phases available for a project.

The project manager should pursue the options and choices of which project methodology to use, depending on the engagement. Tables 3.3 and 3.4 reflect similar methodologies available to project managers when working with a client and deciding which approach to adopt.

For numerous SDLC-type projects today, the trend and style of these methodologies frequently involve completing one phase after the next. Many are monolithic in nature; they are

Table 3.2 Simple approach

Phases	Phase Description	Critical Plans
Discovery	Researches and refines organizational objectives for the project.	Strategy/roadmap
Design	Provides the design and solution to the organization.	Blueprint design
Construction	Constructs the product against the design blueprint.	Project plan
Implementation	Implements the tested solution into the organization.	Test/deployment
Follow-up	Ensures that solution is rolled out smoothly and irons out issues.	Maintenance

time consuming and some methodologists are calling these formal giants the dinosaurs of project methodologies. SDLC methodologies at least provide a framework for completing projects, but it's not that these methodologies follow the often-quoted maxim "Ye shall release early and release often"; rather, they rely on "Ye shall wait till each phase is complete before releasing resources for the next." In today's complex digital world, where faster is better, project managers struggle to complete

Table 3.3 Complex approach

Phases	Phase Description	Critical Plans
Definition	Identifies the project team and lists assumptions.	Project schedule
Data collection	Collects data for the intended solution.	Analysis forms
Develop model	Develops a conceptual model of the solution.	Specification
Verification and validation	Confirms that solution performs as required and compared to all measurable results.	Validation plan
Optimization	Ensures that the solution meets predefined success criteria.	Optimization plan
Delivery	Delivers the solution to the client.	Deployment plan

Table 3.4 Generic approach

Phases	Phase Description	Critical Plans
Needs analysis	Determine exact client requirements.	URS, Business case
Project concept	Establish business objectives and deliverables from the client.	Project definition
Project design	Start designing the solution for the client.	Specifications
Training	Provide training to users in the client organization.	Training plan
Project delivery	Implement the project per the identified project schedule.	Deployment plan
Project support	Address all support-related aspects of the project.	Support plan

projects where complex, unknown technologies are being used. Clients *do* want to see results much earlier than before. They insist that you follow a project approach, but they want to see results much more quickly and want deliverables to be delivered sooner. My advice is to go through the various approaches mentioned here and select one that is best suited for your needs, and tailor it accordingly. In addition, refer to Chapter 4 of this book to start a journey into methodologies (see Figure 3.6).

➤ Approach

➤ *Needs analysis.* This phase is used to determine the specific client requirements for the proposed solution. The needs analysis aids in identifying the exact business and functional requirements.

➤ *Project concept.* The project concept establishes the business objectives and assumptions, risks, and deliverables into a project concept, which is usually documented and presented to the client for acceptance.

➤ *Project design.* This phase allows the project design or development team to begin creating or formulating the design for the solution.

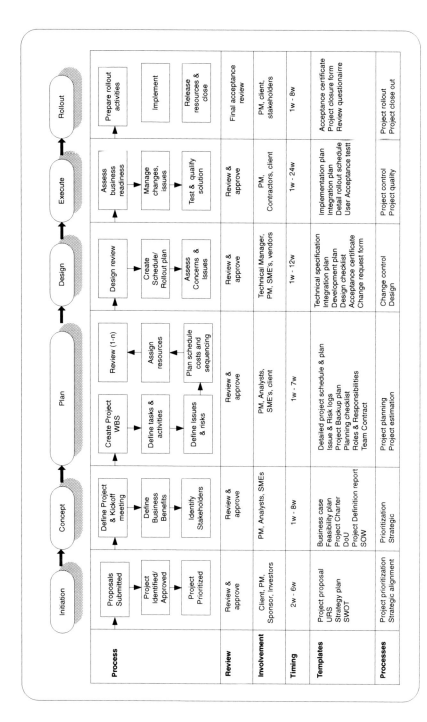

Complex Project Life-Cycle Methodology

	Initiation	Concept	Plan	Design	Execute	Rollout
Process	Proposals Submitted	Define Project & Kickoff meeting	Create Project WBS	Design review	Assess business readiness	Prepare rollout activities
	Project Identified/ Approved	Define Business Benefits	Define tasks & activities	Create Schedule/ Rollout plan	Manage changes, issues	Implement
	Project Prioritized	Identify Stakeholders	Define Issues & risks	Assess Concerns & Issues	Test & qualify solution	Release resources & close
			Review (1-n)			
			Assign resources			
			Plan schedule costs and sequencing			
Review	Review & approve	Review & approve	Review & approve	Review & approve	Review & approve	Final acceptance review
Involvement	Client, PM, Sponsor, Investors	PM, Analysts, SMEs	PM, Analysts, SME's, client	Technical Manager, PM, SME's, vendors	PM, Contractors, client	PM, client, stakeholders
Timing	2w - 6w	1w - 8w	1w - 7w	1w - 12w	1w - 24w	1w - 8w
Templates	Project proposal URS Strategy plan SWOT	Business case Feasibility plan Project Charter DoU Project Definition report SOW	Detailed project schedule & plan Issue & Risk logs Project Backup plan Planning checklist Roles & Responsibilities Team Contract	Technical specification Integration plan Development plan Design checklist Acceptance certificate Change request form	Implementation plan Integration plan Detail rollout schedule User Acceptance testt	Acceptance certificate Project closure form Review questionairre
Processes	Project prioritization Strategic alignment	Prioritization Strategic	Project planning Project estimation	Change control Design	Project control Project quality	Project rollout Project close out

Figure 3.6 Complex life-cycle methodology.

➤ *Project training.* The training phase is an important part of this methodology because it includes training as part of the project. It assumes that training for the user is necessary.

➤ *Project delivery.* The implementation of the project occurs after training has taken place. This phase ensures that the project is delivered at the relevant location(s) within schedule.

➤ *Project support.* This phase of the project ensures that the necessary support for the solution has been coordinated and managed. Tasks such as support level agreements (SLAs), escalation processes, and contact lists are performed.

■ SOLUTIONS-BASED PROJECT METHODOLOGY

Solutions methodologies offer consulting companies the opportunity not only a way to work with clients but also a structured manner in which to deliver projects. They form the standard approach to doing the work. As each solution is different from the rest, it becomes important to adhere to a consistent manner in which projects are managed and executed.

Ray Lane of Kleiner Perkins Caufield & Byers states:

> E-business is about rebuilding the organization from the ground up. Most companies today are not built to exploit the Internet, their business processes, their methodologies, their hierarchies, the number of people they employ . . . all of that is wrong for running an e-business! (p. 1)

There are numerous e-commerce project and development methodologies available today. They vary largely because of their architectures, technology, and target dates. At a minimum, e-solutions methodologies should consist of the following phases.

➤ Objectives.

➤ Strategy.

➤ Design.

➤ Content.

➤ Development.

➤ QA.

➤ Test.

➤ Launch.

➤ Maintenance.

➤ Creating a Basic Methodology

If you are new to methodologies, you should start with a simplistic approach for your project. The first step is to list a few key phases you think suit your type of business. In the following example, we start building a methodology. Assume you have a small project team in your company and that your aim is to avoid any lengthy documentation or additional steps that will impede project delivery. You can always start elaborating as your project starts gaining momentum. For the purpose of the example, I have randomly selected three basic phases of our methodology:

1. *Explore.* Here you need to ensure that the focus remains on completing the business requirements for the upcoming solution. This includes obtaining project information, meeting with your client, and creating a list of assumptions and a project brief or business case. You should drill down into some level of analysis and determine what the project scope is or is not.

2. *Develop.* During this key step, start creating at least the project plan, together with any technical specifications you need to build your product. This may include case diagrams and flowcharts. Additionally, during this phase, the role of the deployment plan is highlighted.

3. *Execute.* During the execution phase, the physical solution is developed and tested to the point where the solution is rolled out to the client.

With the main phases documented, we need to identify the minimum artifacts or project templates needed. Table 3.5 shows that we need at least a business case document during the "explore" phase. After you have the templates defined and in place, assess which processes you need to support this methodology. Assume that your company or project will be purchasing considerable hardware and services from different vendors. In this case, you need to ensure that you have a procurement and financial process in place to make things easier. If these basic processes are not in place, it is likely that you will be spending more time doing administrative work than managing your project.

After the processes have been identified and established, run a simulation or demo to see that everything works the way that you designed it to work. Tweak the methodology by either adding or deleting pieces to the methodology. If your company or project is small, you want to be flexible and able to communicate to fellow team members in an efficient manner without any complexity. Many companies make the fatal mistake of having reams of documentation do the communicating between parties instead of face-to-face communications. But our example is fine. We have kept the methodology to a minimum set of templates and processes, and we have our project team sitting together in a comfortable and relaxing work environment.

As our team or project becomes larger, it will require additional coordination and, regrettably, slightly more documentation. In addition, depending on the technology, we want a highly dynamic project environment that can create this solution quickly (e.g., we want to create a national database that

Table 3.5 Solutions-based models

Basic Phases	Phase Description	Basic Artifacts Needed
Explore	Examine the deliverables needed, as well as resources.	Business case
Develop	Develop solution against specification.	Technical specification
Execute	Implement the solution.	Deployment plan

collects and interprets intelligence data from multiple government agencies).

■ CREATING HYBRID METHODOLOGIES

There are circumstances in which it may be necessary or appropriate to combine two methodologies to create one perfect tailored methodology. Sometimes, it is more feasible to dynamically build a methodology from other methodologies. You may find yourself starting out using a waterfall methodology, then during the life cycle of the project (i.e., development), you realize that using a RAD methodology may be more appropriate. Remember that each methodology offers its own set of strengths and weaknesses from a methodologist's perspective. In the Air Force, to keep mission-critical aircraft serviceable, the "one–from-two" principle is sometimes employed—two unserviceable aircraft are stripped down and critical parts are used to build one fully functional aircraft tailored for a specific use. This is the concept of the hybrid approach.

For any project manager, this option should remain open, but with sudden change comes risk. Points of safe cutover from one approach to the other must be clearly defined, and the project manager should assess the impacts on schedule, cost, and resources. There are issues with the user involvement in the different streams of development, project management issues including possibly different approaches to change requests in the two approaches, and organization management issues. This is permitted, provided the project management framework in the company can support various development methodologies (see Figure 3.7).

■ SUMMARY

Some of the project methodology steps you use will be collapsed or expanded, depending on the project (i.e., more process or less process). Some super projects require so much definition and business detail that they require much more use

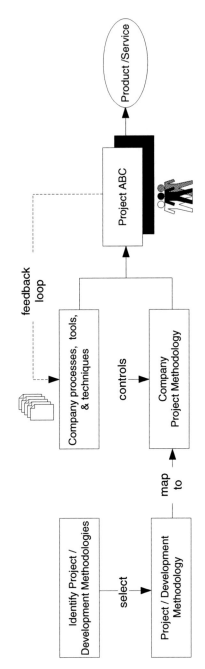

Figure 3.7 Selection process for project and development methodologies.

of templates and supportive processes, while shorter projects are simple and to the point, not requiring as much definition and use of templates, and could be finished in weeks. You must learn to adapt. By default or design, all project methodologies adhere to a similar universalized project management discipline. However, the methods and tools differ, as follows:

➤ Regardless of the size or scope of the project, you need to apply a consistent project methodology to ensure the highest standards of excellence.

➤ Accountability throughout all stages of the project is essential. At key project milestones, the project manager presents its progress for client review and approval. Consistent review maximizes project efficiency and ensures customer satisfaction.

Miyamoto Musashi (2000) states:

You should not have any particular fondness for a particular weapon, or anything else for that matter.

Figure 3.8 is a clear-cut example of a documented project management methodology. It shows three distinct phases to follow, with a listing of key project documents to use for each phase.

■ LESSONS LEARNED

1. Don't underestimate the time it takes to develop and maintain consensus and commitment to the new project management methodology and the changes it involves. It takes time to adjust to the approach.

2. When assessing a company requiring a new project methodology, identify the bottlenecks and concerns of users.

3. Build an efficient "open" communication system into your methodology. Without it, you are prone to difficulties and stronger coordination.

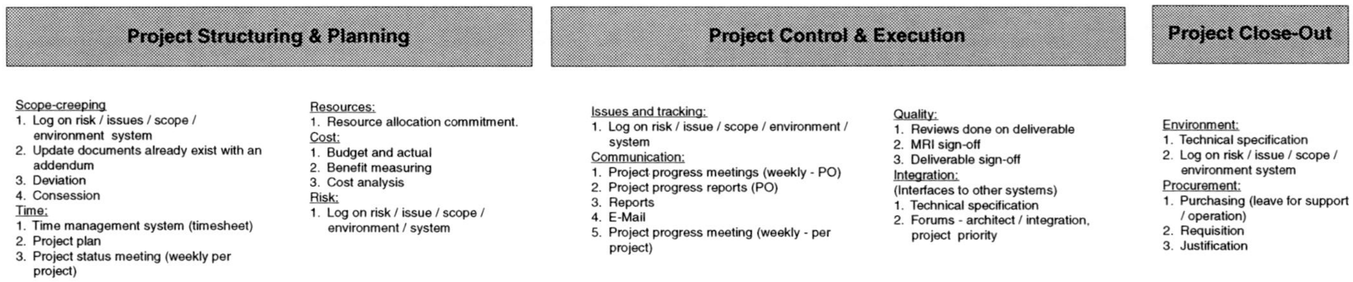

Project Structuring & Planning

Scope-creeping
1. Log on risk / issues / scope / environment system
2. Update documents already exist with an addendum
3. Deviation
4. Consession

Time:
1. Time management system (timesheet)
2. Project plan
3. Project status meeting (weekly per project)

Resources:
1. Resource allocation commitment.

Cost:
1. Budget and actual
2. Benefit measuring
3. Cost analysis

Risk:
1. Log on risk / issue / scope / environment / system

Project Control & Execution

Issues and tracking:
1. Log on risk / issue / scope / environment / system

Communication:
1. Project progress meetings (weekly - PO)
2. Project progress reports (PO)
3. Reports
4. E-Mail
5. Project progress meeting (weekly - per project)

Quality:
1. Reviews done on deliverable
2. MRI sign-off
3. Deliverable sign-off

Integration:
(interfaces to other systems)
1. Technical specification
2. Forums - architect / integration, project priority

Project Close-Out

Environment:
1. Technical specification
2. Log on risk / issue / scope / environment system

Procurement:
1. Purchasing (leave for support / operation)
2. Requisition
3. Justification

Figure 3.8 Simple methodology design.

4. Do not mistake methodologies for tools. The deployment of new tools for project management might lead to the wrong belief that a database could substitute for sound project management practices.

5. Beware of being too definitive with the new system. Some learning of the best way to use the system should be allowed, because all new opportunities cannot be predicted in advance, and users should have an opportunity to learn and establish good habits. Some of the project managers have useful skills and good practices, which should not be lost in the new system.

6. Recognize that people who have already bought in to the new system may opt out when they realize its impact on their existing working practices. The new system results in changes in practice, roles, and responsibilities, as well as in changes to job boundaries. As the impact of changes is gradually appreciated by those affected, the willingness to cooperate is significantly increased if the project manager handles the changes with tact and sensitivity.

7. When designing a methodology, try to reduce the amount of complexity and administration.

8. Be sure to explain vaguely expressed concerns. A new project management methodology must be backed up by, and integrated with, training in the necessary project management areas and clear messages about its significance for the business.

9. Demonstrate tangible results quickly to show people how the new methodology and tools will help them to deliver projects more efficiently.

10. Understand your client's industry when selecting or designing a project management framework.

11. Set your client's expectations correctly—ensure you deliver what they need.

12. Technologies change; therefore, ensure that methodologies are maintained.

■ QUESTIONS

1. Name five objectives when selecting an enterprisewide project management methodology.

2. What is the difference between a *project methodology* and a *development methodology?*

3. If you evaluate your project with the client and he or she states that the project took too long, do you think that a standard waterfall approach was a probable cause? Discuss.

4. Name five best practices for selecting or deploying project methodologies.

5. Discuss the rationale that *one* methodology does not fit all projects.

6. Is PRINCE2 suitable for non-IT projects?

7. What does the term *project strategy* mean? Is it the same as a *business strategy?*

■ REFERENCES

Beedle, M., M. Devos, Y. Sharon, K. Schwaber, and J. Sutherland. "SCRUMA: An Extension Pattern Language for Hyperproductive Software Development." In *Pattern Languages of Program Design,* edited by N. Harrison, B. Foote, and H. Rohnert, Reading, MA: Addison-Wesley, 2000.

Buzan, T. *The Mind Map Book—Radiant Thinking,* London: BBC Books, 1995. p. 29.

Cockburn, Alistair. *Methodology per Project* (October 1999): TR 99.04.

Khosla, Vinod. "GigaTrends," *Wired.* Available from http://www.wired.com/wired/archive/9.04/optical_pr.html.

Malik, Palencia. *Synchronize and Stabilize versus Open Source, Computer Science* report 95.314A. Ottawa, Ontario, Canada: Carleton University (December 6, 1999).

Musashi, Miyamoto. (T. Cleary, Translator). *The Book of Five Rings.* Boston: Shambhala Publications, 2000, April 2001.

Newman, P. "OGC, PRINCE2." Available from www.ogc.gov.uk/prince/.

Royce, W. "Managing the Development of Large Software Systems," *Proceedings of IEEE WESCON,* 1970. pp. 1–9.

Royce, W. *The Rational Edge—CMM versus CMMI, From Conventional to Modern Software Management,* February 2000.

Senge, Peter. *The Fifth Discipline—The Art and Practice of the Learning Organization.* New York: Doubleday/Currency, 1990.

Using the Rational Unified Process for Small Projects; Expanding upon eXtrme Programming. Gary, Indiana: Gary Police, Rational Software.

van Onna, Mark M. *Progress in Changing Environments with PRINCE2, THS—Worldclass Guide,* January 2000.

Weaver, P., N. Lambrou, and M. Walkey. *Practical SSADM,* Ver. 4, 2nd ed. Pitman Publishing, 1993.

Development Methodology—Selection and Utilization

■ USING DEVELOPMENT METHODOLOGIES

In this chapter, we explore various development methodologies used on projects either alone or in conjunction with a bigger project framework. Most project work can be a chaotic activity, often characterized by the phrase "fighting fires." The project is often started without much of an underlying plan, and the designs are often changed because of technology or error. Sometimes the project is simply cobbled together from multiple quick-paced decisions. This can be effective if the project is small, but as the project grows to be a medium- or super-sized project, it becomes increasingly difficult to add features to the system. The project manager's coordination skills are tested to the fullest extent as the project gets larger. Furthermore, mistakes become increasingly prevalent and difficult to fix (i.e., change control, issue logs). For example, building a space vessel begins with a blueprint based on numerous aeronautical and mathematical calculations, including material specifications, variables, and tolerances. Any change to this blueprint, which must be followed at all times, can kill the project because changes are costly and schedules can be horribly affected. The tools and materials that were manufactured specifically for the space vessel project are very expensive and should not change during the construction phase. On such a project, everything needs to be predictable.

Alternatively, when we look at developing software, we see something very different. We obviously try to build new software solutions—usually with new technologies—therefore, the associated risks are very high. In comparison to building space vessels, developing software is not the same. One is predictable and the other is not. In this chapter, we look at predictable methodologies, then at nonpredictable ones.

■ HOW MANY DEVELOPMENT METHODOLOGIES ARE THERE?

There are no one-size-fits-all development methodologies. Some companies have their own unique customized methodology for developing products or services; others simply use standard commercial off-the-shelf methodologies. With the incorrect methodology, discovering, designing, building, testing, and deploying projects can be chaotic. At least 20 different methodologies are competing to be the best methodology, and this list of methodologies keeps on growing (see Figure 4.1).

The project methodology that is chosen represents merely the framework for the real work to be done and indicates where creativity is needed. Many times, project managers simply select the available methodology and continue to develop their projects with that same methodology. When unpredictable results occur on a project, they raise issues and risks and try to manage reactively. Project managers often lack the controls to measure and respond to the unpredictable. Therefore, they must first determine that the methodology is the correct one.

Many project managers find it difficult to give up control as provided in traditional development. There is no guarantee that the team will deliver if you just follow a chosen methodology. Clients seldom complete requirement specifications because their requirements are constantly changing. The most

Methodology /Life Cycle	Risk	Ease to Implement	Resource Intensive	Frequent Changes	Easy to Manage	Scope Creep	Reliability	Document Oriented	Project Approach
Open Source	Low	Easy	(3 icons)	✓	✓	✓	✓	X	Iterative
XP - Extreme	Med	High	(1 icon)	✓	✓	✓	✓	X	Iterative
Pharma	Med	Average	(3 icons)	✓	X	✓	✓	X	Phased
Object Orientated	High	Difficult	(4 icons)	✓	X	✓	✓	X	Iterative
Spiral / MBASE	High	Difficult	(4 icons)	X	✓	✓	✓	✓	Phased
RAD	Low	Easy	(1 icon)	✓	✓	X	✓	X	Phased
Crystal	Med	Easy	(3 icons)	✓	✓	X	✓	X	Iterative
Incremental	Med	Average	(3 icons)	X	✓	✓	✓	✓	Phased
Prototyping	Low	Easy	(1 icon)	✓	X	✓	✓	✓	Phased
UniCycle model	Low	Easy	(1 icon)	X	✓	✓	✓	X	Phased

Figure 4.1 Assessing project development methodologies.

logical solution is to simply evolve the product as the client's needs change along the project development process. This shows the need for a methodology more flexible than a formal waterfall approach. In fact, the trend is shifting to the more iterative or incremental style of methodologies.

Most project developments are wrongly approached with the assumption that the methodology used is well understood, and the project can be easily planned and estimated. When a project begins to fail, the development process is immediately provided with more resources and attention to get it back on track. Thus, cost and schedule overruns start occurring. These step-by-step approaches do not work because they do not cope with human and technical unpredictability. Rigid processes are often too constraining and fall short of delivering a project to operations or production.

➤ Influence of New Product Development

In today's progressive marketplace, every moment counts. Companies developing new products, whether new bridge construction or a wireless mobile device, usually do so concurrently with existing product developments, often competing for similar resources and delivery dates. These projects must be developed in a synchronized approach with some differentiator toward the development of new stellar products. Hence, a competitive project methodology is needed that can show value and reflect the corporate strategy goals and objectives. The project team, armed with the right tools, techniques, and methodology, can keep the client involved and improve the bottom line. The methodology can be adjusted to fit the solution. The Standish Group's landmark 2000 report, "Chaos in the New Millennium," reports that outright project failures declined from 40 percent to 23 percent during the past five years but challenged projects swelled from 33 percent to 49 percent in the same period. Reasons listed included cost overruns and projects with lower functionality than promised. The correct choice of methodology plays an important part in elevating the rate of failures (see Figure 4.2).

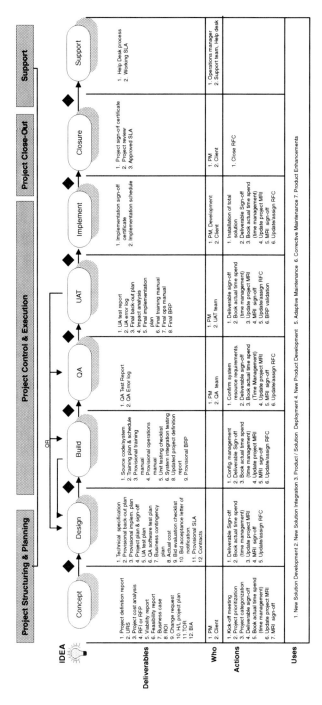

Figure 4.2 New product development process.

99

➤ Requirements for Selecting a Methodology

Table 4.1 illustrates essential decisions a project manager must make when selecting a methodology:

> ➤ *Budget.* Budgets play a big role in any project, and the type of methodology to be used is key. For example, you have been given a mandate to develop a product within eight months. Your sponsor says, "Money is no problem; we need this product by the end of the year." If you select a *heavy* methodology, you may not achieve your goal because you will see the results only near the end of the project. (Earned value could possibly help, too.) A *light,* agile methodology may be the more appropriate choice because many of the lightweight methodologies are done in iterations and budgeted accordingly. If the project appears to be failing, funding is discontinued; if the iteration proves successful, funding for the next release is approved and work continues.

Table 4.1 Requirements for selecting a methodology

Requirement	Rationale
Budget	Methodologies require money and effects schedule.
Team size	Number of staff to be managed is required.
Project criticality	The urgency of the project decides the methodology.
Technology used	Hardware such as computer servers, composite materials, or electronics may be needed.
Documentation	The methodology needs documentation.
Training	Effective training to key support staff and project managers is required.
Best practices/ lessons learned	Past lessons learned and good practices should be available.
Tools and techniques	Tools and techniques must be available.
Examination of existing processes	The maturity of existing processes will influence the pace at which a project will progress.
Software	Methodologies require software as part of their design.

➤ *Team size.* Methodologies are directly proportional to the team size—use light methodologies for smaller teams and heavy methodologies for larger teams. Projects with teams of 100 members geographically dispersed throughout the globe will not work using a small, lightweight methodology. The lines of communication grow more complex with the increase in team size, necessitating a more disciplined, coordinated model. For example, the Boston Big Dig project, the largest underground artery roadwork project in U.S. history—estimated at $14.5 billion for 7.5 miles of highway—requires thousands of workers across many vendors and employment agencies. A lightweight methodology is not suited to such a project.

➤ *Technology used.* The technology used on a project affects the direction and type of methodology selected. Unfamiliar technology slows progress. On many projects today, simulation and testing of new technologies is actually considered a phase of the methodology.

➤ *Tools and techniques.* Some project methodologies require more tools and techniques than others—for example, databases, visual modeling tools, and project management tools; some require hardly anything. If a project manager must manage multiple design changes, he or she will need a configuration management tool and technique.

➤ *Project criticality.* Any critical project with a "must-deliver" target date needs to have the correct choice of methodology. The project might require additional resources to finish by the required date. If the methodology is too small, the project manager loses control; too large and formal, he or she slows the project down. A project manager's experience and skills will help in choosing the best approach.

➤ *Existing processes.* In any company, the maturity and ease of use of existing project processes largely influence the methodology. Some company processes may be totally unreliable and ad hoc, slowing down completion of tasks. For example, you follow the standard internal purchasing process, which has a lead time of two months to receive goods. This process requires intervention or change.

No two methodologies are ever quite the same. At last count, my research on this topic found 45 different methodologies. If you don't have any methodologies in place in your company, on your next project, begin documenting issues and steps. Each major event (e.g., design) symbolizes either an end to a phase or the beginning of the next phase. All phases have unique activities and deliverables from previous activities. Before moving to the next phase, make sure all the activities and deliverables are completed. If you don't, expect to have more problems than usual.

■ UNDERSTANDING LIGHT AND HEAVY METHODOLOGIES

The choice between using a light or heavy methodology determines the success of the project.

➤ Light Methodologies

Ever-increasing technological complexities, project delays, and changing client requirements brought about a small revolution in the world of development methodologies. A totally new breed of methodology—which is agile, adaptive, and involves the client every part of the way—is starting to emerge. Many of the heavyweight methodologists were resistant to the introduction of these "lightweight" or "agile methodologies" (Fowler 2001). These methodologies use an informal communication style. Unlike heavyweight methodologies, lightweight projects have only a few rules, practices, and documents. Projects are designed and built on face-to-face discussions, meetings, and the flow of information to the clients. The immediate difference of using light methodologies is that they are much less document-oriented, usually emphasizing a smaller amount of documentation for the project. For example, they are somewhat code-oriented: The team considers the source code as the project documentation. Advantages of a lightweight methodology include:

➤ It works well with change.

➤ It is people-oriented rather than process-oriented. It works *with* people rather than against them.

➤ The methodology is complemented by the use of dynamic checklists.

If a client constantly introduces frequent changes to the design to see what the solution will look like—possibly to see immediate results or functionality of the product—a light methodology may be the suitable route to follow. Although you might set some limits to prevent too many changes, in today's ever-changing technological environment, clients might prefer that the project proceed in smaller iterations. The great thing about light methodologies is that they are learning methodologies. After each build or iteration, the team learns to correct issues on the project and improvement cycles form throughout the project. Additionally, with light methodologies, the project teams are smaller and rely on working more closely, fostering knowledge sharing, and having almost instantaneous feedback. The project manager does not need to develop heavy project documentation, but should instead focus on the absolute necessary documentation (i.e., project schedule).

➤ Heavy Methodologies

The traditional project methodologies (i.e., SDLC approach) are considered bureaucratic or "predictive" in nature and have resulted in many unsuccessful projects. These heavy methodologies are becoming less popular. These methodologies are so laborious that the whole pace of design, development, and deployment actually slows down—and nothing gets done. Project managers tend to predict every project milestone because they want to foresee every technical detail (i.e., software code or engineering detail). This leads managers to start demanding many types of specifications, plans, reports, checkpoints, and schedules. Heavy methodologies attempt to plan a large part of a project in great detail over a long span of time. This works well until things start changing, and project managers inherently try to resist change.

If the project manager does not obtain a complete list of user requirements from clients for the heavyweight project, it's very likely that the heavy methodology will not work effectively because the project will be racked with change, slippages, and rework on the project documentation. A heavyweight methodology works on the assumption that the more rules and coordination there are, the better the project result will be. A complex project requires sufficient documentation just to jog the memory of the many team members on the project. However, excess methodology is very costly and inept—there are more updates to reports, plans, and schedules. Alternatively, there are times when a heavyweight methodology may be appropriate for super projects where it is necessary to gain stricter control and coordination between phases, and to improve the lines of communication between team members.

Any project with a team larger than 10 to 20 people who work in multiple locations may be a good candidate for a heavyweight methodology. Many companies are simply rushing to try to come up with the biggest and best methodology—including the most templates. Many, expecting miraculous results, become disappointed after a few months of actual project work. Because technologies are becoming more complex and integrated—facing many design and development problems—heavyweight methodologies can sometimes be the best choice, especially when multiple teams are working at different locations and when tighter control and formalization of key parts of the project is necessary.

■ DEMYSTIFYING ITERATIVE DEVELOPMENT

Project managers or developers often confuse the meaning or use of the terms *incremental, evolutionary,* or *iterative.* Incremental, iterative, and evolutionary development are in fact the same thing. They execute all project phases (i.e., design, build) more than once. Whereas linear development (i.e., SDLC) is not. On any project, team members must understand the difference in these terms because they can define the future course of the methodology being selected or proposed on the next project. Iterative development adds agility to your project. For example, if you start a project and the executive sponsor informs you to follow an iterative approach, would you know what the sponsor meant? The following analogy best describes the differences in terminology:

➤ *Iterative.* When building a house, the first iteration of the house is torn down, redesigned, and the second iteration is built from scratch. The emphasis is on re-doing the project. In the construction industry, this can be impractical and expensive; but in the information technology industry, this approach is common.

➤ *Incremental.* When building a house, we start off with a basic design, and then incrementally add more rooms to the house. The emphasis is on *adding to the project* or expanding it. In addition, incremental models are best used to do a *phased delivery* to clients (e.g., release 1, release 2). This approach is more orientated to formal projects such as construction projects; information technology projects also use this approach as a dynamic way of delivering projects to clients.

The main difference between the iterative and incremental approaches is that you can still live with the incrementally built house, but the iterative house that has been torn down needs rebuilding.

➤ Benefits of Iterative Development

The iterative development methodology provides the following benefits:

➤ It encourages user feedback, which promotes obtaining real user requirements.

➤ The system grows by adding new functions to each iteration.

➤ Developers or planners start focusing on the biggest issues or risks facing the project.

➤ Any misconceptions about design and requirements are identified upfront.

➤ Everyone on the project has an accurate snapshot of the project status as it progresses.

➤ Continual testing is carried out during the project.

➤ The project workload is spread more evenly over the life cycle.

➤ It allows for lessons learned on prior versions to be used in future releases.

The project or development manager divides the development/design schedule into a few iterations (e.g., iterations 1, 2, 3, 4, 5, and 6). Each iteration is one to four weeks. The iterative approach now forms the basis for everything forward. Iterative approaches need to be managed slightly different from a normal project, as each iteration is built on its specific set of user requirements at that time. As iteration 1 is completed and reviewed with the project team and client, another iteration is planned wherein additional requirements and functionality are built into subsequent iterations. Each iteration concentrates on capturing the client's most pressing tasks. Instead of creating a detailed schedule, iterative methodology project planning should be more dynamic—each iteration is planned as it comes along, with smaller planning windows.

■ THE AGILE METHODOLOGIES

Project or development managers are still facing controversy between the agile and heavyweight methodologies. Currently, many companies favor the agile methodologies. Agile methodologies present new, nontraditional ways of building complex products and systems. Projects that use agile methodologies are now starting to report improved time line and cost savings, compared to those in the heavyweight family. Additionally, project teams are hailing the agile family of methodologies as remarkable because, at last, a series of methodologies contributes directly to the business. Many managers (i.e., functional, project, and development) tend to stick with the heavyweight methodology because they want to predict the entire project until the last man-hour, whereas the project teams (i.e., developers, coders, analysts) tend to stick with dynamic shorter cycles. Industries that use agile methodologies include financial, IT, telecom, utilities, and many more service industries. Furthermore, this trend is starting to emerge worldwide. The following are the most commonly used agile methodologies:

➤ Extreme Programming (XP).

➤ Scrum.

➤ Crystal methodology.

➤ Dynamic Systems Development Methodology (DSDM).

➤ Rapid Application Development (RAD).

➤ Adaptive software development.

➤ Lean development.

➤ Feature-driven development.

Agile methodologies better suit small projects where smaller project teams are involved. With larger team size and the complexity and duration of the project, the choice of a heavyweight methodology is purely from a command and control perspective. Many smaller companies do not use heavyweight methodologies and prefer the more agile approach to building solutions.

➤ Extreme Programming (XP) Methodology

XP, one of the new promising breeds of lightweight methodologies, is the brainchild of Kent Beck. XP is one of the agile processes. It has received so much attention in recent years that some of the global project organizations are reviewing it for inclusion in their methodology portfolios. XP has few rules and a modest number of best practices, which are all relatively easy to use. It is based on iterations that embody several practices (like RUP), such as small releases, simple design, testing, and continuous integration. XP also promotes several effective techniques for the appropriate projects and circumstances; however, there are hidden assumptions, activities, and roles. XP teams use a simple form of planning and tracking to decide what should be done next and to predict when the project will be finished. XP embraces four core values that its project teams should follow: (1) communication, (2) feedback, (3) simplicity, and (4) courage.

The focus is on business value, where the team produces the software in a series of small, fully integrated releases that pass all the tests the client has defined. An XP project defines an integrated set of practices, which requires the full-time, on-site engagement, for such a project to work successfully. XP concentrates on construction of code—programming to meet a business need. How that business need occurs—and how it is modeled, captured, or reasoned—is not XP's primary concern. The XP phases are for planning purposes but the focus is on actually building the code. There is little emphasis on project documentation—XP is a clean and focused environment, which allows developers both creativity and freedom during development. The focus of XP is to reduce development costs. Although XP is worthy of consideration as a development methodology, it should not be used on large projects.

XP is a more constrained process that needs additions to make it fit a complete development project. For a small project team working in a relatively high-trust environment where the user is an integral part of the team, XP can work extremely well. Some of the most noteworthy XP practices are:

> *Refactoring.* Restructure the system continually, without changing its behavior, to make it simpler or add flexibility. Determine if this is a good practice for the team. What is simple to one may be complex to another.

➤ *Testing.* Developers continually write tests to go along with their code. The tests reflect the stories. XP urges you to write tests first, which is an excellent practice because it forces you to deeply understand the stories and then to ask more questions when necessary. Whether before or after code, you have to write them. Add them to your test suite and make sure to run them every time the code changes.

➤ *Pair programming.* This technique ensures room for two developers to work effectively at a single workstation. This results in better code in less time, because developers can identify errors and possible faults in the software code (*Strengthening the Case* 2000).

➤ *Use CRC (class, responsibility, and collaboration) cards.* This advocates that spending time to capture and maintain design documents is fundamental to a project's success. XP projects typically require a few hours to sketch the design or use CRC cards. The cards are used to teach users of XP the principles of object-orientated design.

XP can be used in conjunction with other development frameworks. XP has been successfully used with Rational Corporation's RUP. This combination has been called the *dX process* and is also RUP-compliant (Martin, nd).

➤ The Scrum Methodology

In the agile community is a *light* methodology developed by Jeff Sutherland. The name *Scrum* comes from the game of rugby, played by two teams of 15 players with an oval ball. The ball is carried in the hand and may be passed backwards or laterally across the pitch or kicked in any direction. The opposing players attempt to halt the ball carrier by tackling him or her with their arms. Points are scored by:

➤ Touching the ball down over the opponent's goal line (a *try*, worth 5 points).

➤ Kicking the ball above the crossbar and between the up-rights of a large H-shaped set of posts. This may be done either from a place kick following a rule infringement (a penalty goal) or a kick from the hand, provided the ball strikes the ground before being kicked (a drop goal). Both types are worth 3 points.

➤ A conversion, which is attempted after a try has been scored and is similar to a penalty goal except worth only 2 points.

The purpose of the scrum is to restart play quickly, safely, and fairly after a minor infringement or stoppage. From a methodology perspective, Scrum refers to the mechanism used in rugby for getting an out-of-play ball back into play. Scrum is a lightweight, agile methodology focusing on software development. Scrum's two pillars are team empowerment and adaptability:

➤ *Team empowerment.* When teams are given work to do, they are responsible for figuring out how to do it. The team does the best it can during each increment. While a team works, its only interaction with management is to tell management what is getting in the way and needs to be removed to improve productivity.

➤ *Adaptability.* Scrum uses "punctuated equilibrium." The team maintains equilibrium during each increment, insulated from outside disturbance. Increments are punctuated every 30 days so that the team and management can evaluate what should be done during the next increment; this decision is based on what the team has accomplished and what the environment dictates is the next most important thing to do.

Scrum's ultimate goal is to deliver as much quality software as possible within a series (three to eight) of short time boxes (fixed-time intervals) called *sprints* that typically end every 30 days. Each stage in the development cycle (requirements, analysis, design, evolution, and delivery) is now mapped to this sprint(s). The traditional development stages are retained for convenience, primarily for tracking milestones. For example, the requirements stage may use one sprint including the delivery of a prototype. The analysis and design stages may take one sprint each while the evolution stage may take anywhere from three to five sprints. Defined and repeatable processes work only for tackling defined and repeatable problems with defined people in defined environments.

Before any sprint is started, you define the required functionality for that specific sprint and then allow the project team to develop and deliver it. At the end of every 30 days, the project manager inspects the results, assesses changes in the business environment, and empirically determines what to do next. The goal is to stabilize the requirements during the sprint. Each sprint operates on a number of work items called a *backlog*. As a rule, no more items are externally added into the backlog within a sprint. Internal items resulting from the original preallocated backlog can be added. The goal of a sprint is to complete as much quality software as possible but, typically in practice, less is delivered.

The project manager or executive does not leave the sprint after completion; he or she remains engaged throughout until all the sprints are finalized. The project team holds daily project meetings—called a *Scrum*—in which the team quickly runs through the activities for the following day. The following items typically arise from the scrum meetings:

➤ Potential management blockages and problem areas.

➤ Action items for management.

➤ Overall status of completed items to date for the sprint cycle.

Each sprint takes a preallocated amount of work from the backlog. The team commits to it. As a rule, nothing is added externally during a sprint. External additions are made to the global backlog. Blocks resulting from the sprint can also be added to the backlog. A sprint ends with a demonstration of the new functionality. Scrum meetings typically take place at the same time and place every day; therefore, they serve to build a strong culture. As such, Scrum meetings are rituals that enhance the socialization of status, issues, and plans for the team. The scrum master leads the meetings and logs all the tasks from every member of the team into a global project backlog. Scrum meetings allow the development team to "socialize the team members' knowledge" and have a deep cultural transcendence. At the end of each sprint, there is a demonstration to:

➤ Show the client what's going on.
➤ Give the developer a sense of accomplishment.
➤ Integrate and test a reasonable portion of the system being built.
➤ Engage the team.
➤ Ensure real progress—reduction of backlog, not just the generation of more documents.

After gathering and reprioritizing leftover and new tasks, a new *backlog* is formed and a new *sprint* starts. In contrast, Scrum allows us to build *softer* software, so there is no need to write full requirements up front. We should recognize that *it is impossible* to have full requirements specified upfront or to freeze the context and environment. Requirements are written in a context. Our system transforms that context. New problems arise in the system and the new context (see Figure 4.3).

Scrum is a knowledge-creating process with a high level of information sharing during the whole cycle and work progress. The keys to Scrum are deciding the completion date for production or release, prioritizing functionality, identifying available resources, and making major decisions about architecture. Compared to more traditional methodologies, the planning phase is kept short because we know that events require changes to initial plans and methods. Scrum uses an empirical approach to development where interaction with the environment is not only allowed but also encouraged, thereby changing the scope. Table 4.2 provides a summary of the Scrum methodology.

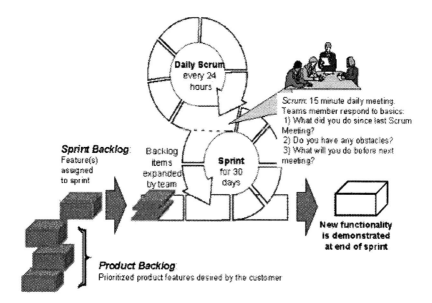

Figure 4.3 Scrum methodology. *Source:* SCRUM, Adaptive Development Methodology, SCRUM © 2002. Used with permission of the Agile Community.

Project management for a Scrum methodology involves a much greater focus on iteration and release management, error and fault resolution, and coaching the team to the next project release. Compared to traditional project management, we see that its sole focus is primarily on producing PERT

Table 4.2 Scrum demystified

Agile, lightweight process to manage and control development work.

A wrapper for existing engineering practices.

A team-based approach to iteratively, incrementally develop systems and products when requirements are rapidly changing.

A process that controls the chaos of conflicting interests and needs.

A way to improve communications and maximize cooperation.

A way to maximize productivity.

Scalable from single projects to entire organizations.

A way to detect and cause the removal of anything that gets in the way of developing and delivering products.

---

charts, Network diagrams, status reports, and deliverables. The most immediate benefits of Scrum are shown in Table 4.3.

Scrum is, therefore, based on empirical controls through inspection and adaptation. These controls are implemented through five basic practices:

1. *Iterations.* All work is done in short iterations, usually lasting 30 days. Inspections occur at the end of each iteration.

2. *Increments.* An increment of working functionality is produced at each iteration. At the end of each iteration, this increment is inspected.

3. *Emergence.* Complex systems emerge unpredictably across time. Their end state can be anticipated but not predicted. It is useless to try to predict their end states, and any such predictions can be misleading. Scrum deemphasizes traditional definitions of the requirements, architecture, and design of the system. These factors are allowed to emerge across time and have successfully done so on thousands of projects.

4. *Self-organization.* There are many unpredictable factors in IT development, ranging from technology to personnel.

Table 4.3 Scrum benefits

Increases user involvement in the development process.

Allows users to change and create requirements as the project progresses.

Ensures that the most important user functionality is built in first.

Always focuses on only the most important functionality.

Achieves new working functionality every 30 days.

Allows the user to choose the "build" or release at any time.

Eliminates the need for projects to be funded more than 30 days in advance.

Identifies something that can be done to improve productivity every single day.

Maximizes the ROI from the project.

Ensures that the team focuses on building only the functionality the user wants, eliminating additional functionality or cost.

Given this unpredictability, it is important that management and teams are provided with the authority to plan and organize the work as they proceed, using their creativity and intellect to deal with the unexpected. They rely on their experience. They may also use any of the documented, defined development approaches (i.e., use case capturing, objcct modcling techniques) that they think will benefit the project.

5. *Collaboration.* The practice and working environments of agile methodologies work only if everyone collaborates freely and openly with one another. Techniques used here are (1) open working environments and (2) paired programming practices.

➤ Crystal Methodologies

The Crystal methodology is a family of methodologies, which are all lightweight in nature and are segmented, as the name implies, into various color bands a crystal would emit (i.e., crystal clear, yellow, orange, maroon, blue, and violet). All Crystal methodologies are founded on a common value, "*very strong on communication, they are human-centric, light on work products and are self-adapting*" (Cockburn 2000). Methodology elements can be reduced to the extent that running software is delivered more frequently and interpersonal communication channels are richer. The human-centric approach really focuses on enhancing the work of the people involved on the project. Each member of the Crystal family or methodology addresses different project needs. The focuses of Crystal methodology are to (1) capture those components that make projects successful and (2) provide the project team with sufficient leverage and freedom to perform its work in a fun and creative manner. Additionally, smaller project teams develop better results because the communication is improved largely through close personal interaction and feedback between users, and the team is encouraged. Crystal does not encourage vast amounts of project documentation. Crystal captures the lessons learned from previous development projects, including the latest briefings on human thinking and communication, which is then reapplied to the development environment. The founder of the Crystal methodologies, Cockburn, states:

> . . . Software development is a cooperative game, in which the participants help each other in reaching the end of the game—the delivery of software. . . . (p. 1)

When the project team starts developing the software, the team members immediately embark on describing their own development vocabulary in a manner that each project member understands. Two main principles of Crystal are:

➤ Put people in the same location for improved development and creativity.

➤ Encourage face-to-face communications.

➤ Dynamic Systems Development Methodology (DSDM)

The DSDM, developed in the United Kingdom, is based on Rapid Application Development (RAD) that uses prototyping reiteration to deliver projects. This model has several aspects that differ from most common models. The difference is that time and resources are fixed and functionality of the deliverable is variable. In other models, the functionality (or product) is fixed, and resources and time are, to a certain extent, flexible.

Businesses today focus on finding the right solutions quickly. DSDM provides a project framework to make this objective achievable. DSDM's goal is speed—but not at the expense of quality. DSDM is independent, ensuring that it is adaptable to meet the needs of any organization. The simplicity, practicality, and flexibility of the approach are suitable for vendors, SMEs, consultants, and so on, making DSDM relevant across a variety of industries.

During the functional model iteration, first-pass descriptions of the new or changed processes are produced for refinement. A pilot project is developed during the design and build iteration. Throughout the development, feedback is used to evaluate and refine the processes so that they can be rolled out to the wider development population with confidence that they will achieve the benefits expected of them.

Implementation of processes involves significant communication and training of the project staff. Because communication is important throughout the development of improved processes and their final delivery, a communication strategy is added to the usual DSDM product set.

The structure of process improvement teams is described based on the DSDM roles and responsibilities. As always, the visionary role is an important one in keeping the focus of the work aligned to the needs of the organization.

➤ Rapid Applications Development (RAD) Methodology

Sometimes users just want to see a product they can understand and not have to wait for the development to get off the build line. Traditional software development methodologies usually follow a sequence of steps with formal sign-offs normally at the end of each project phase. This sequence might be:

1. User requirements are gathered.
2. Specifications and the design are formulated.
3. Development begins and the project is completed.
4. Testing commences.

This process can be time consuming, but RAD shortens the approach.

But what happens if you discover during the development phase that the technology doesn't work? This has immense repercussions for the entire linear approach, and such a methodology could very well cause the project to fail. The time elapsed between the design and development could run into many months or man-hours. Clients are then often unwilling to take such a loss unless it is part of their key business strategy. Project managers need to employ a far more dynamic approach or project methodology for technologies that are untested or fall into a high-risk category. The RAD methodology may be the most suitable to realize immediate benefits.

Compared with many traditional methodologies, RAD compresses the analysis, design, development, and test phases into a dynamic series of short iterative development cycles. RAD uses shorter project phases, which means that benefits are realized much more quickly. With RAD, each iterative development cycle delivers a functional version of the proposed solution. The approach is almost cyclic in nature. However, many organizations don't have the time to spend lengthy periods on development; they want to see immediate results. By following a RAD methodology, clients are able to use a "building block approach" to see the results. Using RAD, results are almost immediate and the product starts becoming tangible. The developers have the advantage of building on their solution and gradually improving it until it reflects what the client requires. Some characteristics of the RAD methodology are:

> ➤ Development teams are much smaller than normal.
> ➤ The development team is integrated (i.e., analysts, developers, testers) and dedicated to the project.
> ➤ The development phases are shorter, cyclical, and extremely dynamic.
> ➤ Each release of a RAD version includes actual functionality the client needs.
> ➤ Releases do not represent entire prototypes; rather, they are usable working systems.
> ➤ Tasks and activities are performed concurrently rather than sequentially.
> ➤ RAD makes use of changing technologies and quick decisions.
> ➤ The entire approach is based on incremental changes, ultimately ending in a quality product.
> ➤ The project team understands that frequent changes are part of the job.

See Figure 4.4 and Table 4.4 for examples of the RAD methodology.

Throughout a RAD methodology, it is important for the project manager to understand that a process needs to be followed. Key steps that need to be emphasized are:

➤ *Analysis.* On RAD projects, it is crucial to interview all the various management staff in the client's organization (i.e., sales, marketing, legal, procurement, billing) for their requirements and objectives. These managers may see higher value in certain areas, and this needs to

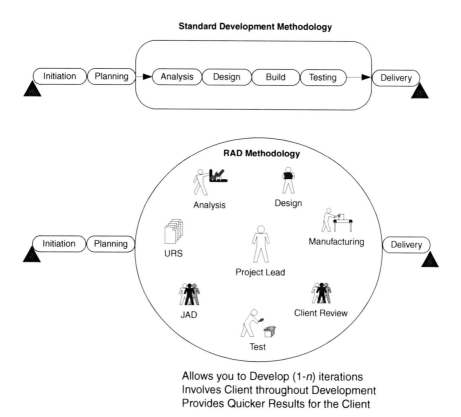

Figure 4.4 RAD methodology.

Table 4.4   RAD methodology

Category	Example
Data warehousing	SAP solution
Customer relationship management	Sales force automation (SFA) solution
Legacy applications conversion	Conversion of old mainframe systems to newer platforms
E-commerce applications	Web site development

be captured in the user requirements statement (URS). (An electronic copy of the URS template is provided on the accompanying CD.)

➤ *Business model.* When the analysis is completed, the task of putting together a business model is of the utmost importance. Here the project team relies on the analysts to formulate and create various options based on the client's intended strategy. This may include the types of reports needed, financial data, and even the workflow for the solution. (An electronic copy of this business case template is provided on the CD.)

➤ *Integration.* Integration of RAD solutions into existing platforms and legacy systems is challenging; therefore, the RAD project team needs to work closely with the client's technical team to capture any business rules or integration issues that would contribute toward a successful integration of the new solution. The well-known software vendors have, to a great extent, already addressed integration into their software. However, if the required solution cannot integrate with certain systems, some customization and development may be needed. This is where the true nature of RAD reveals itself. It goes through various iterations and is repeated until the solution can integrate into the client's organization.

➤ *Documentation update.* Because of the iterative nature of RAD, it is wise to maintain and update all project documentation on a regular basis as the versions are changed and new versions are tested. Proper configuration management of not only the project documentation, but also the source code and database instances, will keep the project under control.

RAD prototyping can reduce costs. It allows the project manager and the team to identify risks early during the project life cycle. The approach overlaps project phases. However, one of the biggest concerns found with RAD is with quality assurance during the development of the project. Project managers, therefore, must ensure that quality assurance is built into the project.

■ THE UNICYCLE METHODOLOGY

The unicycle model is a classic methodology still used successfully today. Before using this model, a feasibility study establishes the justification for the project. Figure 4.5 shows that the project phases are closer than other methods and join in the center, which reflects project communications. The following phases are used:

➤ *Project feasibility and justification.* After the project manager becomes familiar with the project feasibility report, he or she should ensure that the findings are valid and updated. The project manager determines the feasibility for the project during this phase.

➤ *User requirements.* As with all projects, client requirements are mandatory. Some level of effort is required to determine all user requirements. The project cannot continue until this phase has been completed.

➤ *System design.* When the user requirements have been specified and approved by the client and the project team, the project commences establishing a high-level design of the main functions of the proposed solution. The system design will decompose this high-level design into manageable parts.

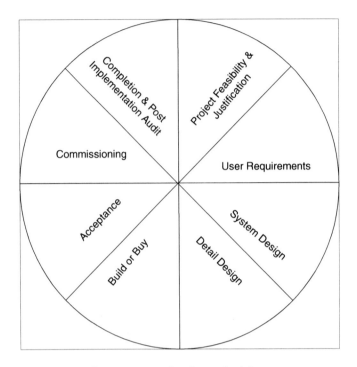

Figure 4.5   Unicycle methodology.

➤ *Detailed design.* After the project team has established the high-level design, a detailed design is prepared. The detail is captured in the project work breakdown structure (WBS) and the design documentation.

➤ *Buy or build.* In many cases, depending on the level of detail, the design, and available resources, it may be necessary to buy the solution instead of developing it. This business-driven decision is made and implemented by the client.

➤ *Acceptance.* All aspects of the solution need to be proven fully functional, documented, tested, validated, and acceptable to the client. This can be achieved through testing.

➤ *Commissioning.* The commissioning is the actual commencement or deployment of the tried and tested solution. The client and users are provided with the necessary training. After all aspects are resolved, formal acceptance is agreed on.

➤ *Completion and postimplementation audit.* Closing the project involves ensuring that project resources are dissolved and released to their organizations. The postimplementation audit consists of performing a thorough project audit after a period of three to six months into its operational steady state. The audit provides many lessons and can be shared with other projects.

■ THE CODE-AND-FIX APPROACH

Code-and-fix is the most common of all development methods in the information technology environment. Code-and-fix is traditionally the methodology used to develop software applications. Additionally, the code-and-fix approach is the fastest and least efficient way of developing applications because this approach often gets out of control and ends up in trouble. There are literally no rules to code-and-fix, as IT developers find ways to skip corners and ignore key development steps. However, in a small startup company with only a few developers, this is often the way projects are managed. The recommendation for such a methodology is to gradually introduce key development templates, checklists, and controls into the development process.

■ V-METHODOLOGY

The V-Model framework is a structured testing approach that can be used with any project management or system development methodology (see Figure 4.6). The framework emphasizes quality from the initial requirements stage through the final testing stage. It focuses on testing throughout the development life cycle, early development of test requirements, and early detection of errors. Each major deliverable in the development process is assessed, verified, validated, and

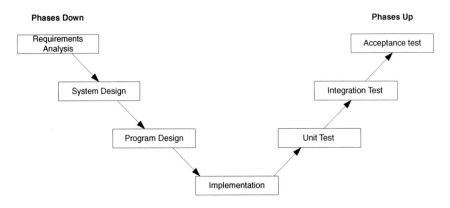

Figure 4.6 V-methodology.

tested. Work proceeds to the next stage in the V-Model when all project deliverables in a stage have met all verification and validation requirements. The process of verification and validation is an attempt to catch as many errors as possible in the development life cycle, otherwise know as *stage containment*.

■ THE WATERFALL METHODOLOGY

The waterfall model originated in 1970 largely through the efforts of Dr. Winston Royce who developed this model as an aid to software development. It worked well at the time and has undergone many subsequent changes and revisions. From 1974 to 1976, Dr. Barry Boehm, a knowledgeable expert in his field, further developed the waterfall model into other project phases to better reflect current development best practices. The methodology, currently one of the most widely used, gets its name from the analogy of water falling downward.

The waterfall model is a diagrammatical representation depicting the main phases of software development (see Figure 4.7). The first phase and its associated action are shown at the top left-hand corner of the diagram, and all subsequent project phases are placed toward the bottom right of the diagram. Each phase is called a *work product*. At the end of each phase, the

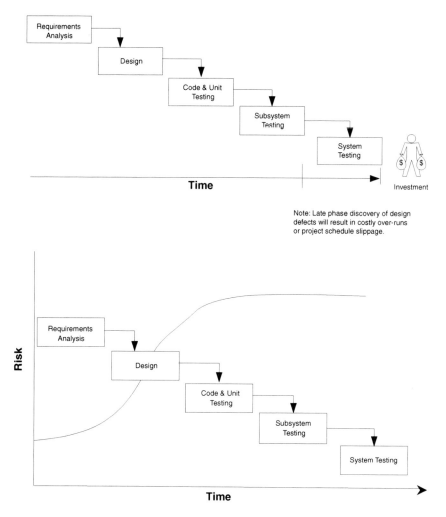

Figure 4.7   Waterfall development methodology.

result is either documents or deliverables, which in turn are used to proceed to the next phase.

Note that the model in Figure 4.7 does not adequately allow for fixing any defects. It also does not address how to revisit previous project phases and go up the waterfall again when defects need to be corrected. This poses problems for some design and development groups. Although a great methodology, the waterfall model is difficult to use because it is incomplete in its original framework and structure. Revisions to the waterfall methodology have been made to accommodate project feedback, such as testing and quality assurance. However, the most commonly used version available today includes a corrective feedback mechanism. Figure 4.7 shows a remarkable difference between the two models. Some of the phases that should be used in the waterfall methodology follow:

➤ Requirements analysis.
➤ Design.
➤ Code and unit testing.
➤ Subsequent testing.
➤ System testing.

There are three main types of waterfall methodologies to consider when assigned a project. These three waterfall approaches depend entirely on a project's target date. These categories are:

1. *No overlap.* This is a purely sequential waterfall methodology where no phases overlap. Phases are completed before another phase starts. Usually, deliverables such as phase sign-offs and reviews are indicators of such a methodology.

2. *One phase overlap.* Adjacent phases are allowed to overlap by one phase only. This kind of overlapping often happens on a waterfall project.

3. *Overlapping phases.* Extensive overlap is present, with each phase overlapping the other. It does prove substantially more difficult to coordinate the deliverables and tasks and requires a competent project manager with the appropriate experience to undertake such an approach. If you run into trouble here, it is difficult to get back on track and requires rescheduling.

The disadvantage of the waterfall methodology in general is that it can be largely documentation-driven, which consumes time. The waterfall methodology makes it easier on the project manager and difficult on the client. For example, in a typical construction project, the specifications are usually detailed and take considerable time to complete. The first time a client actually sees the finished product is when the product has been built. (However, in construction, CAD software can simulate large projects.) Thus, if the client has changes, it is either usually too late or the changes are too complex.

➤ Benefits of a Waterfall Methodology

The following are benefits of a waterfall approach:

- ➤ It provides phase-by-phase checkpoints for the project.
- ➤ You may need to proceed to only the following phase after the previous phase has been completed.
- ➤ It can also be applied to an iterative approach (see Figure 4.8).

➤ Disadvantages of a Waterfall Methodology

Disadvantages of a waterfall approach include:

- ➤ There is minimal feedback between project phases.
- ➤ You start seeing results only later in the life cycle.
- ➤ Each phase is tracked with far too many hard dates and milestones.

■ THE OPEN SOURCE METHODOLOGY

The concept of open-source software development has only recently gained popularity as a radical approach to developing projects. Two classic examples—the Linux Operating System and Netscape's Web browser—were driven largely because of the rise of the Internet, which proved itself as being an effective

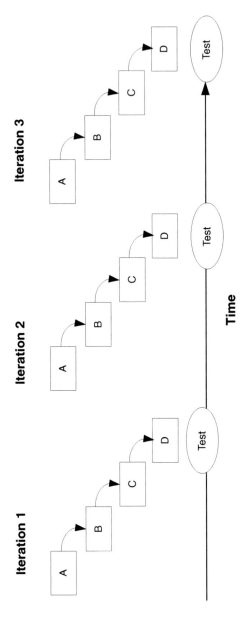

Figure 4.8 Incremental Iterations applied to a waterfall approach. Iteration #1 addresses the greatest risks. Each Iteration produces an executable release, providing more functionality as the iterations develop. Each Iteration must be tested for quality and integration.

communication medium. Developers from around the globe working on open-source projects now communicate with one another using tools such as FTP, newsgroups, developer mailing lists, and e-mail. With open-source, you are not limited to certain projects. Any industry can make use of an open-source model if approached correctly.

The objective of any open-source project is the nonproprietary fashion by which a product's source code is readily shared with any end user using open-source licensing. It is user driven with developers all over the globe becoming part of a user community when working on a specific project. As one developer finishes working on the initial source code and adds to its basic functionality, the source code is passed along to the next member of the user community. Coordination and communication for the project is essential; therefore, project methodology is needed. Concerns of critics of open-source methodology include:

➤ There is virtually no design documentation or other project documentation.

➤ There is no system level testing.

➤ There are no true user requirements apart from basic functionality.

➤ The marketing of the product, when completed, remains incomplete.

The methodology is revolutionary and has had great success to date. A few hobbyist developers initiate and drive the projects. They code-and-fix the source code until it is acceptable to them and then they pass it along to the user community. Figure 4.9 shows the two basic approaches to this method. Approach A starts with a team of developers designing and coding the software. They debug the software until the source code is acceptable. The source code is then released to the general user community, who in turn adds more functionality. The original team plays the role of project coordinators and planners. Approach B starts with a single developer who builds and codes the initial version with the minimal functionality

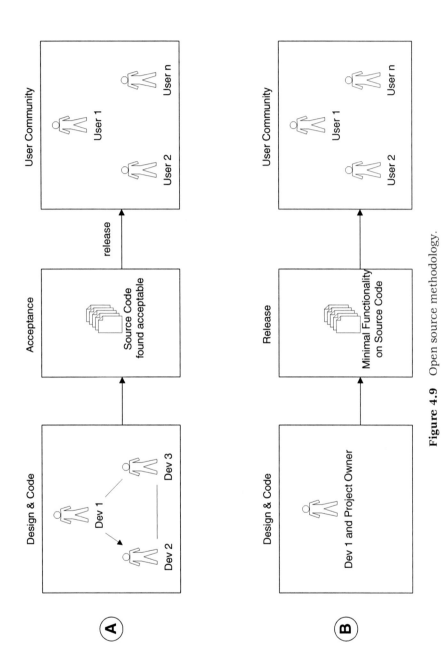

Figure 4.9 Open source methodology.

he or she requires. It is then released to the user community to build further. The original developer becomes the project owner and coordinates the completion of the project.

A typical iteration $(1 - n)$ of an open-source project follows these steps:

➤ The developer carries out the design and code generation—either individually or in a team.

➤ The developers or user community executes concurrent debugging and testing.

➤ New functionality and identified bugs are passed along to the project owner.

➤ A new release is then put together based on the identified bugs and all new functionality that is being requested is reviewed.

➤ When the new release occurs, an open-task list is distributed to the user community, seeking members to voluntarily execute the tasks on the list.

■ THE SPIRAL METHODOLOGY

The spiral model uses a cyclic approach to develop systems by defining the system. This results in various releases. It allows the project manager to build a proof-of-concept for the client early on. The model is rapid prototyping and it centers on evolutionary development, using the *waterfall* model approach for each project phase. With this approach, detail of the entire system is not fully defined at the first attempt. Instead, developers (1) assess the highest priority features, (2) define them, (3) implement them, and then (4) obtain feedback from clients— such feedback distinguishes incremental from predictive development. Based on this flow process, the team goes back and starts to define and implement additional features. Figure 4.10 shows the basic structure of a spiral methodology. The advantages of the spiral model include:

➤ Its design flexibility allows changes at several stages of the project.

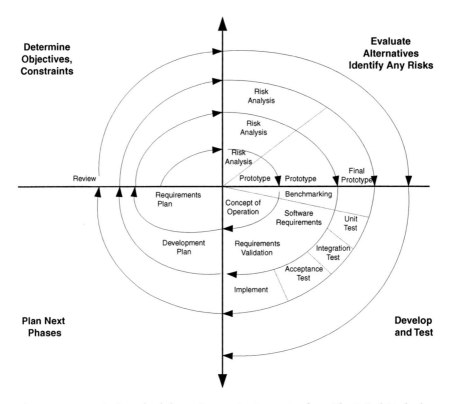

Figure 4.10 Spiral methodology. *Source:* Dr. Barry Boehm, *The Spiral Methodology.* Reprinted with permission.

➤ The process of building up large systems in small segments makes it easier to do cost calculations.

➤ The client, who will be involved in the development of each segment, retains control over the direction and implementation of the project.

➤ The client's knowledge of the project grows as the project grows, so that he or she can interface effectively with management.

➤ The client receives the quality and communication of in-house development.

A spiral model is very much a risk-driven methodology because risk is assessed before each phase and reassessed at

Table 4.5 Solving problems through spiral development

Problems Often Encountered	Spiral Solution
Inadequate user requirements	It enables and encourages user feedback.
Ambiguous communications	Serious misunderstandings are evident early in the project.
Overwhelming architectures	Development focuses on critical business issues.
Subjective assessments	Objective assessment is made through testing and QA.
Undetected inconsistencies	Inconsistencies are detected early in the project.
Poor testing and QA	Testing starts right from the first iteration.
Waterfall development	Risks are identified and addressed early on.

frequent cycles. At times, project managers consider a spiral approach a quick fix approach: "I don't need to develop any project documentation because I'm developing a prototype." There is much more to it than that. A structure still needs to be applied to any RAD project. The spiral model is more difficult than the waterfall methodology but, with practice, its technique and process become easier. An iterative methodology leans more toward the way developers/designers work, rather than the way a project manager would work. There are many variants to the spiral model and even greater strides will be made in the future, but this methodology works well now. Table 4.5 shows various problems that can be solved with a spiral methodology.

■ SYNCHRONIZE AND STABILIZE METHODOLOGY

One open-source model is the one used by Microsoft. The methodology is used to build Microsoft's consumer level products with the synchronize and stabilize methodology (see Figure 4.11). The concept is easy—project team members synchronize their individual/team tasks on a continuous basis and then stabilize the product in small increments, as

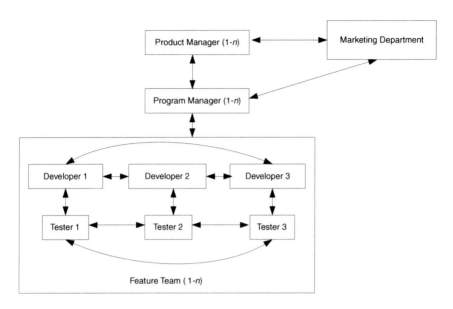

Figure 4.11 Synchronize and stabilize methodology.

the project moves forward. The methodology is based on the phases shown in Table 4.6.

This methodology is feature driven. The team members can work autonomously, thereby ensuring that some creative license is allowed on the project, provided their work can be combined successfully into the daily builds. The teams are also allowed to come up with fun ways of discipline when a daily build has not been achieved. Synchronize (daily build) and stabilize (fix errors at end of each milestone), such that the required set of features is completely functional. Product managers develop a vision statement and feature list based on customer input. Program managers develop an initial functional specification based on the vision statement. Program managers create schedules and parallel feature teams of three to eight developers and testers based on the functional specification.

Table 4.6 Synchronize and stabilize model

Phase	Task	Who
Planning (3–12 months)	Prepare vision statement /requirements assessment.	Product manager
	Develop product specification(s).	
	Project schedule preparation /formulate team.	
Design build functionality (6–12 months)	Design third of the system features— critical features.	Program manager
	Design second third of the features.	Feature team
	Design final third of the features (less critical items).	
Stabilize—fix and freeze build (3–8 months)	Test internally.	Testers
	Test externally.	
	Prepare release.	

■ REVERSE ENGINEERING DEVELOPMENT METHODOLOGY

Important differences with this development model are the inclusion of two conceptually new steps and the reusability of parts of some existing system. As with most models, the development life cycle starts with the requirements. If we get the requirements wrong, we will be developing the wrong product from the start. The requirements of all stakeholders must be considered.

In Figure 4.12, notice the feedback loops. If a test in design fails, design does not move back to performance analysis. A design problem should not be solved by adjusting a performance parameter. Design problems usually go back to requirements engineering, although it is sometimes permissible to check on the functionality on the way. This does not allow a function to be changed without reference to the root requirement. Similarly, if a code fails a test and is subsequently amended, there should always be a back reference to the design of that portion

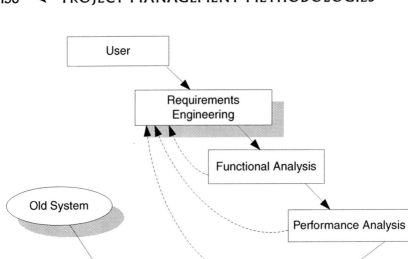

Figure 4.12 Reverse engineering methodology.

of code. Integration and test phase problems should not be rectified by reference to the coding phase but should go to the root at the design phase (then possibly back further). Many projects have been allowed to go horribly wrong by taking "shortcut measures" in the software and hardware developments or accidentally omitting the loop back to the correct place in the development life cycle. Being unprofessional and taking shortcuts do not work and often cause projects to ultimately take more time, not less.

➤ Requirements Engineering Phase

The stages of requirements engineering (RE) are:

1. *Requirements elicitation:* Helping the stakeholder to list and clarify as many requirements as are known.
2. *Requirements analysis:* Listing requirements in logical orders with cross-referencing. This highlights and minimizes duplication, and allows logical grouping of tasks into identifiable areas ready for subsequent action.
3. *Preparation of requirements specification:* Documents the requirements to facilitate further stages.

The deliverable end product from the RE phase is the document known as the *requirements specification,* also called the *operational requirement for contractual action.* This becomes the input document for the next stage—functional analysis.

➤ Functional Analysis Phase

With all the requirements (known to date) laid out in logical groupings in the requirements specification, the next task is to look at the functions involved in each group area. The purpose is to spot duplication of functionality and identify any areas of conflict and contention. For example:

➤ Many stakeholders have had input to the list of requirements, and it is possible that several people have requested the same or similar actions. These duplications of functionality must be sorted out now to eliminate duplication of code and costs later in the development.

➤ Because of the diversity of stakeholder interests, there will be differences of opinion in priority levels among the requirements, with every individual stakeholder claiming that his or her area is more important and a higher priority than others. It is at this stage that the project manager and project development team have to agree on the overall picture for smooth future development.

➤ Not everyone agrees on technical items. The question of who has access and who has write rights can lead to conflict. The project manager and team need to get agreement from the stakeholders. The problems will only get worse if ignored now. Arrange for a conflict resolution meeting where the relevant stakeholders can meet and resolve the issues.

➤ **Performance Analysis Phase**

With all functionality clear and understood by the development team, the next stage is to consider the performance required. Performance indicators include:

➤ Speed of response.
➤ Routing.
➤ Strange effects avoidance.
➤ Choice of hardware.
➤ Preparation for the design stage.

Speed of response to the requirements is the usual way an end user will judge the operational system. When an end user makes an inquiry, he or she expects the whole answer to that inquiry. Some projects allow the response to be a simple message such as "inquiry being dealt with—please wait." The actual processing has taken an unacceptable amount of time, which frustrates the end user and gives the project a poor name. If a requirement states that "the response to an inquiry must appear within x seconds," the performance analysis stage should be sure that it is physically reasonable and technically possible. Stakeholders sometimes make excessive demands. These must be sorted out and agreement reached in this phase.

Routing users through the final system will also be judged as good or poor performance. An end product of the previous stage was a logical grouping of the requirements. Now is the time to start thinking about final performance routing options. Other aspects on which the final system will be judged are how it performs when presented with unexpected input, how it allows the end users to cope with unexpected output, and the error messages and options presented to the end users when strange events occur. This is referred to as *strange effects avoidance.* Now is the time to decide how some of the requirements are to be handled.

➤ **The Final Phases**

The phases of design, coding, and integration are standard to most development models. Testing is carried out within—as well as at the end of—each phase. Notice the loop back from the integration phase goes right to design and not to coding. It is ill advised and sometimes dangerous to attempt to rectify integration problems by altering the code alone.

➤ **Reverse Engineering Phase**

This phase considers any previous system(s) and attempts to reuse existing components. Software, hardware, documentation, working practices, and local standards may all be reused. Any of these that are reliably proven usable are incorporated directly into the new system. Many parts of the old system will not be usable. Other parts may be reengineered via the design phase. The reverse engineering model gets its name from the reusability of previously proven components that are considered relevant to the new development. These components should be reverse engineered via the design phase with only proven components used directly in the new system. The other fundamental differences in this development model are the inclusion of two new phases, namely, (1) functional analysis and (2) performance analysis. The reverse engineering development model can be used for the whole project or on subunits developed individually and integrated into the whole project.

■ GENERAL PUBLICATION METHODOLOGY

Publication houses and documentation-based companies manage their projects differently from the way information technology (IT) or construction companies do. Publication methodologies can be either heavyweight (e.g., books) or lightweight (e.g., creating various magazine iterations). Documentation forms the lifeblood of these companies and schedules become everything.

➤ The Publishing Team

As the manuscript starts moving from rough draft toward a bound book or glossy magazine, project managers are involved with the following team members during the project life cycle.

- ➤ Author.
- ➤ Acquisitions editor.
- ➤ Editorial assistant/project manager.
- ➤ Development editor.
- ➤ Copy editor.
- ➤ Production editor.
- ➤ Typesetter.
- ➤ Indexer.
- ➤ Proofreader.
- ➤ Printer.
- ➤ Graphic artist.

In the documentation industry, extensive use is made of third party contractors for tasks such as writing, typesetting, graphics, editing, indexing, and front cover design. The phases in a publications process are very specialized and demand great patience and challenges to ensure that project dates are met. If a journalist or writer misses a deadline, the magazine, newspaper, or book can be seriously delayed. The process, shown in Figure 4.13, is explained as follows:

➤ *Initiate.* The author submits a manuscript proposal or rough draft to the publishing house for consideration and approval. As with most manuscripts submitted, many are rejected because of market demands. After the acquisition editor has reviewed the manuscript, it is passed to the next phase.

➤ *Development launch.* This phase starts with internal discussion between the acquisition editor, project manager, and development editor, who decide what form and level of quality the project is to take, based on the submitted proposal or rough draft.

➤ *First draft.* A first draft document is sent by the author to the development editor, who makes suggestions on how to make the project take the shape decided at the development launch. The draft with redline suggestions is returned to the author, who incorporates (or sometimes does not) them into the final manuscript.

➤ *Final draft.* A final draft is sent back for comments and verification before production.

➤ *Transmittal package.* A final document is turned into a transmittal package (hard copy of final manuscript, electronic files with author's original coding stripped out, transmittal form, and memo), and is handed over to the production editor.

➤ *Launch meeting.* The production editor reviews the package and calls a launch meeting to discuss the specifics of the project: internal design, author concerns, schedule, and so on.

➤ *Production.* A production schedule and cost estimates are formalized and published internally; freelancers are hired to copyedit, proofread, typeset, index, and illustrate the project. A copyedited version of the manuscript is sent to the author for review; the author returns it with any comments and answers to queries;

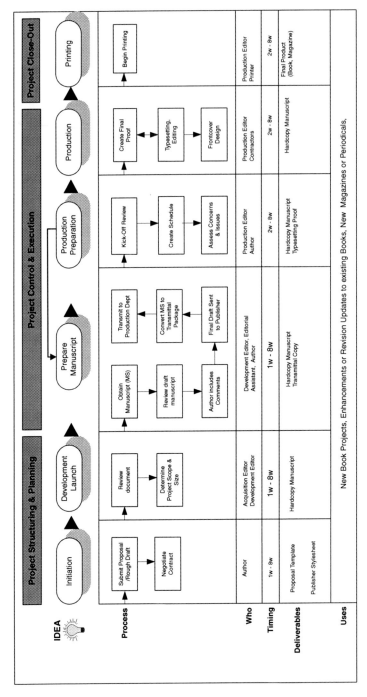

Figure 4.13 Publication project life cycle methodology.

the author's comments are incorporated into the copy-edited electronic files and prepared for the typesetter; the typesetter creates page proofs, incorporating the artwork that was created; and page proofs are sent to the author.

➤ *Proofreading.* Both the proofreader's and author's comments are incorporated into one proof, which is sent back to the typesetter, and a final proof is checked again.

➤ *Printing.* The final electronic files are sent to the printer. Blue-lines are created and sent back to the production editor for approval. The book is then printed.

Although a few concurrent project tasks could occur, in general, one phase needs to be completed before the next phase can start—a typical waterfall approach. More than ever, publication-based methodologies require the following from their project managers:

➤ Time to market is crucial, thus necessitating close coordination of milestones.

➤ Project teams consist of many stakeholders, working across geographic locations.

➤ Project teams need to navigate through many legal and federal hurdles.

➤ Delivery is crucial because many publications have important release dates to the public. If the project is delayed, no one will want to purchase an outdated book or magazine.

➤ The development phases are dynamic.

■ STRUCTURED SYSTEMS ANALYSIS AND DESIGN METHOD (SSADM)

The SSADM is a formal "open" methodology used by the government, private sector, and educational institutions, primarily for IT development projects. This methodology does not address areas beyond analysis and design; therefore, no deployment or implementation is catered for. Launched in 1981, SSADM has been updated and is still in use today. It is an excellent way for developing projects and is not considered a de facto standard.

SSADM is used highly in the IT community and takes a top-down approach to systems development. In this way, a high-level system design is achieved by simply refining the initial system requirements. The aim is to ensure that the design is as accurate as possible and that all requirements have been addressed. SSADM has only a limited take-up by large projects for major IT initiatives. This process is rigorous at times and is bound and controlled by the SSADM structural framework. Figure 4.14 shows how a project proceeds using this methodology. SSADM forces formulation and documentation of the necessary strategy for the project. Additionally, it covers substantial areas such as feasibility study and finalization of the design.

This structured methodology can bring cost savings to a project over its complete life cycle, because so much time is spent on performing a thorough design and analyses. The emphasis is providing the best upstream analysis and feasibility to reduce problems downstream.

The SSADM approach gradually transforms the client's requirements into a well-specified requirements document. The requirements are less ambiguous and are relevant to the business needs because the SSADM approach uses a set of tried and tested techniques, whereas many developments are launched without proper thought.

➤ SSADM Viewpoints and Techniques

The SSADM approach requires three interdependent views of a system being developed:

> ➤ *Functionality/processing.* This assesses the way information and data flows around the system and the processes that will be transformed by it, thereby laying out the functions for the users of the system. The technique used here to depict the processing is *data flow modeling* (a technique for analysis processing).

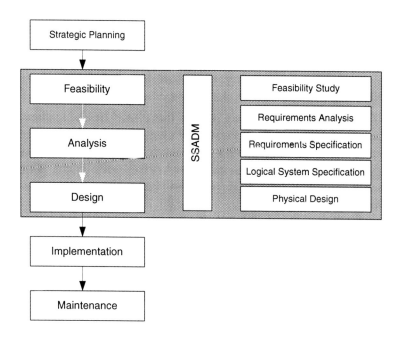

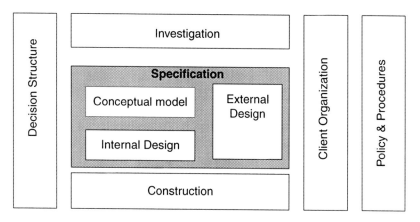

Figure 4.14 SSASDM methodology.

➤ *Data.* The information systems of any organization act as a data store and then act on the data. The data view forms the backbone to SSADM. The technique used here to depict the processing is *logical data modeling* (provides the foundation of the new system).

➤ *Effects of time and events on the data held in the system.* The function and data views are simply "snapshots"; the event view is truly dynamic, as it is specifically designed to model the system behavior over time. The technique used here to depict the processing is *entity behavior modeling.*

The SSADM approach starts with a drawing of a top-level or top-down breakdown of the system into its lower level. It takes three interdependent views of a system that is going to be developed. SSADM is a product-driven methodology because it is largely concerned with completion of the product, along with the quality, rather than the application techniques.

An SSADM project goes from investigation to construction under the influence of the client organizational structure along with their internal policy and procedures. During this development cycle, decisions are made through the decision structure layer. Figure 4.14 illustrates this point.

■ THE PRAMIS METHODOLOGY

The aim of this methodology is to reduce rework and promote earlier problem detection. At the same time, an improvement in the quality of the products produces important savings in the maintenance phase of a project, which means important savings for clients and an improved commercial image of the developer. Customer satisfaction should lead to increased sales. This methodology should be oriented toward the planning and control processes of systems and software development projects. Results would be the enhancement of the quality of the development processes of a particular company and, consequently, enhancement of its guarantee of conformance with the customer's requirements. This methodology also takes into account the ISO 9001 standard.

Over the years, this methodology has been used to deliver projects on time, on budget, and in a way that keeps clients satisfied. This methodology is very flexible, and although not all components of the methodology apply to all clients, as a framework for success, it is unrivaled. A typical process applied to a typical development project follows:

➤ *Phase 1: The discovery phase.* Initial assessment of projects should be given as much consideration as any other stage of the project. While the client usually has a good idea of what he or she wants, it can take the consulting team a great deal of work to understand the internal project language and all the unsaid design goals. Corporate culture can be the enemy of a successful project because all those things you take for granted as "the way things are" may be unknown to your consultants, or subtly different from your end users' beliefs and experience. This model requests that the client agree to a small, fixed cost for discovery tasks. This phase culminates in a detailed requirements specification and more complete cost estimate. There are two distinct deliverables; first is the requirements and implementation plan. This makes no mention of cost and has value as a road map to the completed project. The second deliverable is a quote for the implementation of that plan; it includes the information the client needs to understand the cost and time involved in implementing the project. This is usually done on a short duration, fixed-cost basis, allowing the client and consultant to build a mutual understanding of the tasks and the capabilities of both teams.

➤ *Phase 2: The development phase.* The development phase is typically where the bulk of the project time is spent. This phase implements the project plan developed in the discovery phase, up to the point that the application is feature-complete according to the initial specification, plus any mutually agreed-on changes that have been accepted by both the client and the consultant. This phase can be billed on a fixed-price or time-and-materials (T&M) basis. Billing method depends largely on how well-scoped and definitive the development effort can be.

➤ *Phase 3: Beta test and functional acceptance.* This is the client's first real exposure to the application and will very likely produce change orders. Any misconceptions or omissions from the discovery phase will be most apparent here. Bugs will be found and must be handled. In this phase, projects that get into trouble really begin to show the signs of stress. To reduce the risk associated with this phase, you should agree that work done in this phase be handled on a T&M basis, but at a greatly reduced rate. The low rate produces a general feeling of goodwill, because the customer still recognizes a cost associated with the work, and the consulting organization is disincented from pushing work from Phase 2 to Phase 3.

➤ *Phase 4: Deployment and final acceptance.* Rollout tends to be a fixed cost, one-time expense. Handling this correctly is critical and must be carefully planned. Additional support resources are often required during the rollout phase. A well-planned rollout phase with the right level of support and training can mean the difference between success and failure for the project in the long term. For most users of the finished project, the rollout phase is their first contact with the highly anticipated new tools. Documentation tends to be a fixed cost, but its scope should be clearly agreed on in advance. A predefined set of expectations must exist. The target audience is a critical consideration. Documentation meant for end users in a "How-to" format is vastly different from—and does not replace the need for—technical documentation on the structure and design of the deliverable.

Success is based on quickly assimilating each customer's technical and documentation standards, project procedures, construction processes, supplier requirements, contractual terms and conditions, and preferred contractors and equipment supplier agreements. In many situations, project consultants function as an extension of their client's staff and as an integral part of the project effort. In addition, these teams can add value to the project execution process based on experience, internal company procedures, and knowledge of industry standards. As part of this methodology, project managers must seek to meet your expectations through the use of key review and approval steps.

■ OFFSHORE DEVELOPMENT METHODOLOGY

In considering and implementing any offshore development project, companies are frequently looking at outsourcing those functions of their business that do not make economical sense to develop or maintain locally. This could typically be the development of products internationally—such as building an airport in Hong Kong or developing software in China for a U.S. company. It might even include upgrading a legacy mainframe system into a new Web-based system. Outsourcing must consider the potential vendor capabilities in the possible areas of (1) engineering, (2) manufacturing, (3) information technology, (4) competencies, and (5) support. Projects benefit from the choice of an offshore partner who is able to provide services on a global basis. Companies outsource offshore principally to:

➤ Take advantage of skills the vendor can provide.
➤ Reduce internal conflict with primary corporate business objectives.
➤ Reduce cost of services.
➤ Focus on critical project goals and objectives.
➤ Gain quick access to latest technology.
➤ Gain access to resources that otherwise might not be practical to obtain or retain.

➤ Have access to best-in-class technologies, tools, and processes.

➤ Reduce predictable costs and improve effectiveness.

Companies at this stage have already decided to reduce costs internally, and certain business areas are forecasted to cost even more. The decision to outsource is based on:

➤ Size of the project (too large to do in-house).

➤ Complexity of the project requiring more interactions.

➤ Availability of resources and/or environments and their cost.

➤ Cost of development tools required for offshore development and so on.

A typical offshore project has the following stages:

➤ Project initiation.

➤ Requirement study.

➤ High-level design.

➤ Detailed design.

➤ Construction.

➤ System testing.

➤ Acceptance testing.

➤ Delivery.

Through outsourcing, clients have the flexibility to use (1) people, (2) processes, and (3) technology to enhance, manage, and maintain systems and operations. This can be done remotely from any offshore facility, or co-located on clients' premises. Offshore development methodology stages typically include:

➤ *Application management:* Staff, processes, and methodologies for maintaining, enhancing, and supporting applications.

➤ *Application development:* Staff, processes, and methodologies for developing new applications.

➤ *Business process management:* Services to manage and execute enterprise business processes, including the sourcing and staffing of professionals.

➤ *Help desk:* Provides the professional staff, facilities, and infrastructure to effectively support users of applications and systems. Support services include problem reporting, resolution and tracking, and application usage assistance.

➤ *Operations management:* A set of services that provides real-time management and operation of the information technology infrastructure supporting critical business operations. Typical services include hardware and software configuration, performance management, capacity planning, problem resolution, problem tracking, backup, and recovery.

➤ *Business continuation:* Contingency planning and disaster recovery services required for maintaining business operations in the event of information technology infrastructure failure.

The offshore development methodology has a clear distinction of the activities that can be done on-site and offshore. Of the stages specified previously, the first three stages are normally carried out at a client's site. After the high-level design (system specifications) is complete and signed off by the client, further work on detailed design and construction is executed offshore. The client approves the system test plans. Detailed system test specifications are then prepared based on the approved plan. System testing can be carried out either offshore, on-site, or both. For example, BMW of Munich has many manufacturing plants located offshore (e.g., South Africa), which produce world-class products. Similarly, in the IT industry, more and more companies in the West are starting to outsource their legacy systems in countries such as India, China, and the Philippines.

If external interfaces are not available in the offshore environment, these interfaces are "stubbed" and the rest of the system is tested. These stubs are removed at the client site and the tests are repeated after integrating these external interfaces. Acceptance testing is done by the users who normally provide on-site support during a client's acceptance testing. After completion of acceptance testing on-site, skilled resources can be provided for supporting the implementation. The methodology follows formal structured software development life cycle models and uses the latest structured methodologies while executing software projects.

➤ Benefits of an Offshore Methodology

The added benefits of an offshore methodology are great for organizations that cannot afford to maintain or develop their own solutions or systems at home. In such cases, some of the benefits are:

- ➤ Productivity improvements.
- ➤ Substantial cost savings.
- ➤ Flexible resource base.
- ➤ Large resource base of highly qualified staff.
- ➤ Faster ramp-up of resources.
- ➤ Faster delivery.
- ➤ Extension of the service day (up to 13 hours).

Table 4.7   Prerequisites for using offshore methodology

Prerequisite	Client	Vendor
The technical infrastructure is in place.	✓	
Access to the systems has been resolved.	✓	✓
The project team is able to transfer knowledge.	✓	
Processes and procedures are clearly defined.		✓
Legal and pricing issues are resolved.	✓	
Project management is in place.	✓	✓

➤ Offshore, yet on-site, advantage.

➤ Control and consistency.

Table 4.7 lists the prerequisites for offshore support.

■ GENERAL DRUG DEVELOPMENT METHODOLOGY

Assume you are a successful IT project manager who has been assigned to work for a new client; or you're a consultant and you find employment at a pharmaceutical company, where you are to head up a large multinational team of chemists and doctors to develop a new revolutionary drug. Can you do it? Yes, if you have a thorough grasp of project principles, understand process, and are able to learn quickly.

A new *drug development methodology* is best defined as a process followed for all those project activities and tasks—from the identification of a lead compound to the approval by a regulatory agency—for marketing a new drug. The project management methodology is surely one of the most crucial aspects for taking the new drug development through to its conclusion (see Figure 4.15).

Many drug and pharmaceutical companies rely on the research and development of new drugs to prevent life-threatening diseases and viral outbreaks throughout the globe. Engaging in any new drug project is a comprehensive task and should not be taken lightly. It requires considerable investment and resources, and may take up to fifteen years to get approval by monitoring agencies, such as the Federal Drug Agency (FDA). Even getting the IT systems in place to support the drug development process is audited by the FDA and also requires formal methodologies, which necessitate formal documentation and regulatory requirements.

New drug development is an R&D project, where the risks are notably high and can cost from the tens to hundreds of millions of dollars to develop and market. The research costs are astronomical during clinical trials. Therefore, drug companies want not only the best pharmaceutical and medical

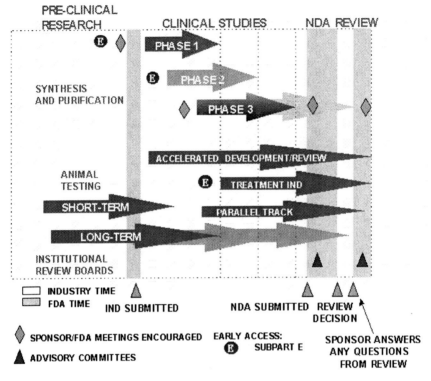

Figure 4.15 New drug development methodology. *Source:* FDA requirements, *Overview of the drug development process,* www.fda.gov/cder/handbook /develop.htm. Reprinted with permission.

minds developing these vital drugs, but also a structured project methodology for this effort. Without a development process, the process simply will not work.

Many drug-related projects face failure because of the high risks and research involved. The success rate is small. After a drug has been registered and approved, the sponsoring drug company will have applied for a patent. Modern-day patents for drugs are limited to a 20-year period, thus limiting their product earnings capability. This leaves manufacturers with only a short time to commercialize and recover the research and development costs before the patent expires. Competitors quickly start developing generic equivalents after the patent elapses and offer the drugs at much lower costs than the original manufacturer, which forces prices down dramatically.

More importantly, these pharmaceutical companies adhere to certain standards and guidelines. The new drug development methodology is an example of such a process. It divides new drug development into the following main categories:

➤ Concept.

➤ Preclinical research.

➤ Clinical studies.

➤ NDA review.

➤ Concept

After a concept has been identified and presented, new compounds must be identified before the project can proceed. Literally thousands of compounds can be selected at this stage, and the concept phase is an important one to consider before moving to the preclinical research phase.

This is the early phase of the overall drug/biologic development process dealing with the synthesis of and search for compounds and the screening processes developed to identify lead compounds. The discovery phases relate to the *research* component of *research and development.*

➤ Preclinical Research

In this phase, chosen compounds are studied to determine their bioavailability, absorption, distribution, metabolism, and elimination. The necessary tests are carried out in cells and in animals to establish preclinical parameters for safety and efficacy.

Under FDA requirements, a sponsor must first submit data showing that the drug is reasonably safe for use in initial, small-scale clinical studies. Depending on whether the compound has been studied or marketed previously, the sponsor may have several options for fulfilling this requirement:

➤ Compiling existing nonclinical data from past in vitro laboratory or animal studies on the compound.

> ➤ Compiling data from previous clinical testing or marketing of the drug in the United States or another country whose population is relevant to the U.S. population.
> ➤ Undertaking new preclinical studies designed to provide the evidence necessary to support the safety of administering the compound to humans.

During preclinical drug development, a sponsor evaluates the drug's toxic and pharmacological effects through in vitro and in vivo laboratory animal testing. Genotoxicity screening is performed, as well as investigations on drug absorption and metabolism, the toxicity of the drug's metabolites, and the speed with which the drug and its metabolites are excreted from the body. At the preclinical stage, the FDA generally asks, at a minimum, that sponsors: (1) develop a pharmacological profile of the drug; (2) determine the acute toxicity of the drug in at least two species of animals; and (3) conduct short-term toxicity studies ranging from two weeks to three months, depending on the proposed duration of use of the substance in the following proposed clinical studies:

> ➤ *Synthesis and purification.* The research process is complicated, time-consuming, and costly; and the end result is never guaranteed. Hundreds and sometimes thousands of chemical compounds must be made and tested in an effort to find one that can achieve a desirable result.
>
>   The FDA estimates that it takes approximately eight and a half years to study and test a new drug before it can be approved for the general public. This estimate includes early laboratory and animal testing, as well as later clinical trials using human subjects.
>
>   There is no standard route through which drugs are developed. A pharmaceutical company may decide to develop a new drug aimed at a specific disease or medical condition. Sometimes, scientists choose to pursue an interesting or promising line of research. In other cases, new findings from university, government, or

other laboratories may point the way for drug companies to follow with their own research.

New drug research starts with an understanding of how the body functions, both normally and abnormally, at its most basic levels. The questions raised by this research help determine a concept of how a drug might be used to prevent, cure, or treat a disease or medical condition. This provides the researcher with a target. Sometimes, scientists find the right compound quickly, but usually hundreds or thousands must be screened. In a series of test tube experiments called *assays,* compounds are added one at a time to enzymes, cell cultures, or cellular substances grown in a laboratory. The goal is to find which additions show some effect. This process may require testing hundreds of compounds as some may not work, but will indicate ways of changing the compound's chemical structure to improve its performance.

Computers can be used to simulate a chemical compound and design chemical structures that might work against it. Enzymes attach to the correct site on a cell's membrane, which causes the disease. A computer can show scientists what the receptor site looks like and how one might tailor a compound to block an enzyme from attaching there. But even though computers give chemists clues as to which compounds to make, a substance must still be tested in a living being.

Another approach involves testing compounds made naturally by microscopic organisms. Candidates include fungi, viruses, and molds, such as those that led to penicillin and other antibiotics. Scientists grow the microorganisms in what is known as a *fermentation broth,* with one type of organism per broth. Sometimes, 100,000 or more broths are tested to see whether any compound made by a microorganism has a desirable effect.

➤ *Animal testing.* In animal testing, drug companies make every effort to use as few animals as possible and to ensure their humane and proper care. Generally, two or more species (one rodent, one nonrodent) are tested because a drug may affect one species differently from another. Animal testing is used to measure how much of a drug is absorbed into the blood, how it is broken down chemically in the body, the toxicity of the drug and its breakdown products (metabolites), and how quickly the drug and its metabolites are excreted from the body.

➤ Clinical Studies

During this phase, the results of the preclinical tests are submitted to the monitoring agency (i.e., FDA) for review before the drug can be tested in humans. An investigational new drug (IND) application is filed and must be approved before any human testing begins. Approximately one in five new IND request makes it to the marketplace.

➤ *Phase 1: Safety studies.* This phase begins trials in humans that test a compound for safety, tolerance, and pharmacokinetics. The Phase 1 trials usually employ normal (i.e., healthy) volunteers and may expose up to 50 individuals to the drug. For most therapeutic biologics and any known toxic compounds, such as anti-cancer agents, only patients with the targeted illness would be used.

➤ *Phase 2: Efficacy studies.* These are the first studies (usually) to define efficacy. In general, 100 to 300 patients enter into various closely monitored clinical trials during this phase. Dose and dosing regimens are assessed for magnitude and duration of effect during this phase. Some companies further differentiate this phase into Phase 2A for studies designed to set dosing and Phase 2B for studies designed to determine efficacy.

➤ *Phase 3: Extensive clinical testing.* These are expanded controlled and uncontrolled clinical trials intended to gather additional evidence of effectiveness for specific indications and to better understand safety and drug-related adverse effects. Phase 3 trials are usually large multicenter trials, which collect substantial safety experience and may include specialized studies needed for labeling (e.g., pediatric or elderly, comparative agents). Phase 3 trials normally include between 1,000 and 3,000 patients.

➤ *Phase 4: Postapproval studies.* This phase is activated or requested only by the FDA when a drug is approved for marketing. There are many reasons for performing Phase 4 studies, including:

—To elucidate the incidence of adverse reactions.

—Large scale, long-term studies to determine the effect of a drug on morbidity or mortality.

—To study a patient population not previously studied (e.g., children).

—Marketing-oriented comparison studies against competitor products.

➤ New Drug Application (NDA) Review

The new drug application (NDA) is the vehicle through which drug sponsors formally propose that the FDA approve a new pharmaceutical for sale in the United States. To obtain this kind of authorization, a drug manufacturer submits an NDA nonclinical (animal) and clinical (human) test data and analyses, drug information, and descriptions of manufacturing procedures.

The project manager should ensure that all the necessary NDA documentation is correct and in good order. An NDA must provide sufficient information, data, and analyses to permit FDA reviewers to reach several key decisions, including:

➤ Whether the drug is safe and effective for its proposed use(s), and whether the benefits of the drug outweigh its risks.

➤ Whether the drug's proposed labeling is appropriate, and, if not, what the drug's labeling should contain.

➤ Whether the methods used in manufacturing the drug and the controls used to maintain the drug's quality are adequate to preserve the drug's identity, strength, quality, and purity.

The purpose of preclinical work—animal pharmacology/toxicology testing—is to develop adequate data to obtain a decision that it is reasonably safe to proceed with human trials of the drug. Clinical trials represent the ultimate premarket testing ground for unapproved drugs. During these trials, an investigational compound is administered to humans and is evaluated for its safety and effectiveness in treating, preventing, or diagnosing a specific disease or condition. The results of this testing comprise the single most important factor in the approval or disapproval of a new drug.

Although the goal of clinical trials is to obtain safety and effectiveness data, the overriding consideration in these studies is the safety of those in the trials. The Center for Drug Evaluation & Research (CDER) monitors the study design and conduct of clinical trials to ensure that people in the trials are not exposed to unnecessary risks.

➤ Typical Drug Project Team

The following team members are required for drug-related projects, which aim to register and approve public accessible drugs:

➤ Doctors.

➤ Biologists.

➤ Biochemists.

➤ Microbiologists.

➤ Chemists.

➤ Pharmacokinetics, formulation, and toxicology expertise and manpower.

➤ Computer modeler.

➤ Project manager.

➤ Project coordinator.

The methodology is a long and often complex series of challenges facing the project team. Project expertise and commitment are needed to make it work. Most importantly, success is built around how the team is led and managed. The project may fail at any stage of the new drug development because of poor efficacy, inability to formulate properly, toxicity, uncompetitive costs, or many other project-related factors.

■ SUMMARY

Just as wireless devices/PDAs today have slowly started to replace connected desktop/laptop systems, we see newer, agile, lightweight methodologies advancing as possible replacements for the more rigid heavyweight methodologies. From the methodologies discussed in this chapter, we see that there are numerous methodologies across all industries—light, heavy, and hybrids. They differ in the number of people involved in the project, the criticality of the project, the project priorities, and, probably, by the personal philosophies of the people involved in these projects. If you didn't find the ideal methodology in this chapter, simply use the best one of all the mentioned methodologies and expand on it. Supplement it with templates and assess the processes needed most. A good development methodology optimizes quality, consistency, and timeliness of delivery.

Whether you use PRINCE2, RUP, RAD, Waterfall, Open Source, Scrum, Spiral, or another, you should be familiar with these underlying concepts. One project may require one approach while another project may need something unique. While projects differ in size and complexity, your unique project approach is based on using key building blocks to understand what needs to be done when designing/using a methodology. These building blocks are:

➤ Understanding and assessment of the engagement and the solution to be implemented. Before initiating an engagement, the project team works to understand the intricacies of the problem. From this flows a comprehensive assessment of the solution to be developed, including time lines and budgets.

➤ Planning the full scope of the project. Based on the assessment, a detailed project plan is assembled. This includes schedules, milestones, staffing, risks, and dependencies. Over the life cycle, the project plan becomes the foundation and framework for all activities.

➤ Team design that assembles the best group of professionals for the job. Project teams are assembled not only based on the technical acumen required, but also on domain expertise in solving specific business problems.

➤ Project management that ensures a timely delivery within your budget. The team relies on a combination of industry best practices and techniques to ensure that projects come in on time and within budget.

➤ Communicate to project teams that any project methodology should follow a structured, yet flexible approach, be able to deliver quality, and ensure client involvement at all times.

■ LESSONS LEARNED

The following lessons are crucial in understanding development methodologies:

1. Simply adopting a methodology is not feasible without a thorough assessment and gap analysis.

2. Don't try to sell a Rolls Royce to an organization that requires only a Jeep. Sometimes they really don't need all the flash.

3. Gaining executive support for moving ahead with a methodology is paramount to the success of any organization. Without executive support, it becomes increasingly complex and time consuming.

4. Determine your business strategy first, and then focus on the tactics you wish to employ.

■ QUESTIONS

1. When dealing with a waterfall methodology, can one proceed with the life cycle if the requirements have not been finalized and signed off on by all parties?

2. Define *heavy* and *light* methodologies.

3. Name the benefits of iterative development on a project.

4. Explain how you would convince your client or organization of the benefits of adopting a project methodology.

5. Does the type of organizational structure affect the efficiency by which projects are managed?

6. List five reasons that most projects fail today.

7. Based on your answers in the previous question, would a project methodology resolve these failures?

8. Describe the difference between the spiral and waterfall methodologies.

■ REFERENCES

Adaptive Development Methodology, SCRUM© 06/28/2002.

Cockburn, Alistair. *Human and Technology Manifesto.* p. 1, 2000.

Fowler, Martin. *The New Methodology, Thought Works,* 2001. Available at www.martinfowler.com/articles.

Hamel, Gary. *Leading the Revolution,* HBS Press, 2000. p. 56.

Martin, Robert. Available from www.objectmentor.com/publications /RUPvsXP.pdf.

Michaelson, G. *Sun Tzu, The Art of War for Managers,* 2001. pp. 7, 14.

Musashi, M. (T. Cleary, Translator). *The Book of Five Rings.* Boston: Shambhala Publications, 2000.

Strengthening the Case for Pair Programming, IEEE Software. July/ August 2000.

Chapter 5

Implementing Project Methodologies

Successful implementation of any project methodology is a project itself. The hard part is to roll it out and make it part of the company's everyday culture. You cannot get everyone to start using the new methodology by simply attaching a few wall charts of the project methodology to cubicle walls and expect results. It could in fact take many months to implement a full-blown project methodology. Many project life cycles require the following:

➤ Automation and workflow.

➤ Ease of use.

➤ Proper methodology documentation.

➤ Acceptance by the entire organization.

There are a dozen consulting and boutique firms that offer to implement project methodologies—ranging from a few thousand dollars to a few hundred thousand dollars—into an organization. Unfortunately, few ever take the greater organization and its processes into account. This book should provide you with enough information so that you can successfully deploy any methodology yourself.

One of the first steps in implementing a project methodology is good planning. Questions that need to be considered before implementing the required project or development methodologies include:

➤ Will we get the best value for the money from this methodology?

➤ How do we build project competencies?

➤ Are the appropriate project management processes and practices in place?

➤ Have we chosen the correct project methodology?

➤ Is it flexible enough to do any size of project?

➤ How does our organization learn and continuously improve from this methodology?

➤ Are we able to measure the project benefits? How do we know this?

➤ Are we getting optimum productivity throughout the life cycle?

Some modesty is necessary before attempting any methodology implementation. Who can speak authoritatively on *all* the issues that are of concern in the implementation of project methodologies?

The only thing that really distinguishes projects from nonprojects is the project life cycle. To develop a broad understanding of the generic discipline of the management of projects, both project managers and executives should address the broad range of issues affecting all stages of the life cycle in all kinds of projects. This is certainly a tough challenge: It requires a substantial breadth of analysis and understanding. Maintaining a coherent conceptual view of the discipline at this broader level is genuinely difficult (see Figure 5.1).

■ CONSIDERATIONS FOR METHODOLOGY ROLLOUT

Some project methodologies focus purely on the technology itself (e.g., Siebel software, SAP, Oracle), while others focus more

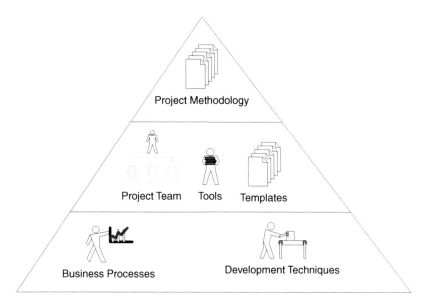

Figure 5.1 Project structure and composition.

on a generic project management approach. You must carefully consider the methodology to use based on the organizational requirements. For example, if you were in the business to build space vehicle systems, you would not be using a Siebel project methodology, but rather a NASA project methodology. A project manager must consider many important aspects before implementing the new methodology. Some preplanning activities that need to be performed before you commence with any methodology implementation include:

➤ Conduct an assessment to understand the organization's current processes, including its strengths and weaknesses.

➤ Determine and prepare a preliminary blueprint to determine the extent to which the organization is willing to employ project management and best practices for other processes (a questionnaire is sufficient).

➤ Develop and tailor the processes with the involvement of the client.

➤ Prepare tools and attach templates to support those processes.

➤ Prepare and implement a rollout and support plan for the new processes.

➤ Train program managers, project managers, and team members.

➤ Mentor program managers, project managers, and team members.

➤ Keep in mind that new processes change the way you work. The key to success in adopting these processes is the manner in which you introduce and deploy them.

Be sure to set a realistic implementation timetable. Project or development methodologies can often spiral when it comes to implementation, if the go-live schedule itself is unrealistic and false expectations are set. Prevailing assumptions about how long methodology deployment should take is sometimes way off base.

➤ **Methodology Selection Matrix**

Because project size and complexity affect the type of methodology to be selected, it is crucial that project managers determine the lay of the land first. Figure 5.2 is a selection matrix, which shows the different sizes (i.e., small, medium, or large) of projects you may encounter. This matrix serves as a useful guide to the type of methodology you should deploy for your project. Selecting the wrong methodology for your project could be disastrous. You will undoubtedly need to make adjustments by either adding or deleting phases.

For example, you are assigned a project that will take 14 months to complete. This project has some integration risk and complexity. By following the vertical axis *complexity*, we select our best judgment guess—*high* complexity. Next, we proceed to the horizontal *time* axis where we select our 14-month range. We then proceed to map the two axes together. We hit a *Large B,* which recommends that we follow a *heavy*

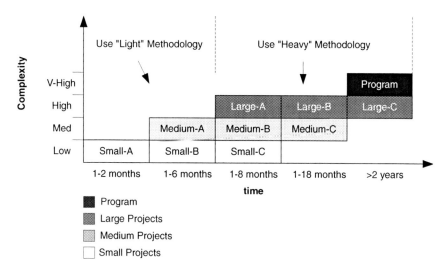

Figure 5.2 Selection of a light or heavy methodology.

methodology. We can trim the methodology down by omitting those parts we don't need.

The same applies to the smaller projects. Assume that your Web site content needs to be migrated from one server to another. By using our matrix, we can determine the choice of methodology for our project. First, on the vertical axis, we agree that the project is low risk (based on the project brief document). We proceed along the horizontal axis and estimate three weeks to complete the project. If we map the axis together, we find that we are in the *Small A* category, which gives us the choice of following a *light* methodology, such as Crystal, RAD, XP, and so on. A heavyweight methodology is too formal and is not needed.

➤ How to Get Started

One of the first things to do is to establish a methodology project team. This team will be responsible for implementing the overall methodology or framework that will be used in the company. After the team has been assembled and briefed on its mission, the team assesses the organization as to the type of business and projects that are generally performed in the organization. A skeleton framework is then developed or created from existing project frameworks available on the market. The methodology is tweaked and adjusted to fit the organization. Next, document and start expanding the methodology. Feedback should be encouraged and used to correct critical issues omitted. After the corrections are made, a pilot project to test the methodology, using a real project, is launched. The following steps should be taken to execute this pilot:

➤ Pilot the implementation processes using a series of workshops.

➤ Establish appropriate project office, portfolio management, and other support functions to enable the new pilot methodology.

➤ Incorporate a process feedback system into the pilot rollout.

➤ Develop a communication plan for the organization.

➤ Measure results continually throughout the pilot implementation.

Many clients do not know what they want when determining project scope, risk, and execution of projects, nor do they realize the intricacies of project/development methodologies. Therefore, the project manager should introduce everyone to the basics of project management or development best practices. After they understand these project/development concepts, show them the need to introduce a framework. Then start extending your efforts by adding project templates, tools, and techniques. The clients at this stage will already have started seeing some tangible results. The aim is to eventually get to a complete package for the client, fully comprehensive and encompassing.

Many of the big five consulting groups use their own unique methodologies when deploying package implementations or projects, in spite of the fact that the clients may have their own methodologies. They do this because following a custom package methodology sometimes doesn't work well by itself, is restrictive, and does not lend itself to being a complete methodology. Therefore, these big five firms combine the best of the best and use their own.

➤ How to Implement the Methodology

First, and most important, the business strategy is reviewed and agreement is reached that there is a need for managing the diverse number of projects in the organization. The methodology should be introduced gradually—it does not help to have a massive deployment to company departments, and possibly operating companies, without first gaining some prior success on a small scale. Implementing the methodology on a step-by-step basis demonstrates early successes and allows you the opportunity to adjust things you may not have had time to do in a single deployment.

As the project lead for the implementation of the methodology, you could decide to conduct a pilot project to prove that the methodology works. You could be faced with a scenario in which a process does not work well, or you might need to tweak a phase of the new methodology. If the project fails because the methodology is too complex or is drawn out because of administrative work, it is time to meet with the project sponsor, who is the champion for the new methodology. Minor issues can be refined based on the pilot project experience. The second project will go more smoothly if you implement what you learned from the pilot project. There has to be some feedback loop built into "tweaking" the methodology.

Additionally, before the pilot project is launched, a select group of identified stakeholders in the company needs to be involved in the introduction process. You cannot simply notify a few key managers. After the stakeholders have been briefed and have bought into the methodology, the team needs to work in a cooperative and collaborative fashion in deploying the methodology. Crucial questions to ask yourself before any deployment include:

➤ What is the purpose of the pilot? What will you achieve/ prove?

➤ What are the project objectives?

➤ In what industry (e.g., pharmaceutical, banking) is the project?

➤ What milestones and deliverables will be needed?

➤ By when should the project be completed (e.g., in two months or two years)?

➤ How many resources are available to complete the project?

➤ Must the project be validated by government agencies (e.g., FDA, EPA)?

➤ What technologies (e.g., high risk, bleeding edge solutions) will you be using?

The introduction of any project methodology to an organization impacts:

➤ The people.
➤ Their roles and responsibilities.
➤ The processes.
➤ The technology being used.

This level of impact must be assessed and managed accordingly. A useful checklist of the issues and concerns should be prepared; it should cover the organization, its culture, the people, and, possibly, attitudes that need to change.

➤ Has a Budget Been Allocated for Implementation?

Successfully implementing a new methodology takes time and considerable resources. There will be costs associated with such an implementation.

For example, a consulting firm tried to implement a full-blown project methodology for a pharmaceutical client. Costs were calculated for only the manpower time for this deployment, but the schedule slipped, and unforeseen costs such as documentation, training, and information technology began driving up the original implementation budget. The project failed because of ineffective budgeting. Some of the most important costs to include in a methodology implementation are listed in Table 5.1.

➤ Implementation Requirements

Certain documentation should be completed before any implementation of methodology takes place. Table 5.2 lists typical documentation.

Table 5.1 Considering rollout costs

Cost Type	Description
In-house resources	Full-time employees assigned to team.
Vendors	Software and hardware acquisition for (1) pilot and (2) production.
Consultants	Needed to bring knowledge to organization on process and project.
Licensing	Annual software licensing fees and support.
Supplies	Color charts, brochures, and project methodology binders.
Traveling	Hotel, meal costs during national or international rollout.
Possible purchase of templates	Templates needed for project phase from industry leaders.
Training	Training users on the methodology.
Support fees	Includes annual support costs to maintain methodology.
Marketing	Web site design or enhancements to marketing brochures.
Shipping costs	Shipping materials and resources to final destinations.

Table 5.2 Implementation requirements

Client Requirements	Yes	No
Solution to guide projects through complete life cycle.	✓	
Sales cycle and operations turnover information.		X
Online application.	✓	
Hardcopy binders with the methodology documented by project manager.	✓	
Complete set of templates for each project phase.	✓	
Accommodations for existing organizational processes.	✓	

➤ Implementation Tools

For many companies globally, the prospect of implementing a full-blown methodology for the first time can be intimidating. In addition, if the implementation team does not understand how the organization's processes work and which tools to use for the actual implementation, things only get worse. I recommend the following tools:

- ➤ Any project management application (e.g., MS Project, Primavera).
- ➤ A spreadsheet to track data and key business information (e.g., MS Excel).
- ➤ Visio Professional or any diagramming application to create flowcharts and processes.
- ➤ Any software development package that allows development of a customized project methodology with graphical user interface (GUI).
- ➤ Workflow software to automate the flow of project deliverables or support the established processes between project teams.
- ➤ An electronic repository for document storage and version control.
- ➤ A sizable database for storing and querying project data.

➤ Implementation Roles and Responsibilities

In any project deployment, a new project methodology rollout requires a project methodology team, which is assigned a project lead. The role players on the deployment side of a methodology pilot rollout, along with their key roles and responsibilities, are shown in Table 5.3.

One of my project manager colleagues planned to sail his boat from Los Angeles Harbor to Honolulu, making the 13-day trip before the hurricane season started. He planned everything well in advance and in great detail. He gathered his five-man crew. A commercial airliner pilot familiar with flight and shipping routes joined as the skipper. A diesel mechanic signed on to manage the engines; he even planned the spare parts to take onboard. A fisherman was a member of the crew—to catch fish should they run out of supplies. The owner of the vessel arranged first-aid training a week before the launch. Everything was planned, from onboard navigation to the handheld Global Positioning System (GPS) system. They set a date to sail but never left. My colleague eventually informed me that in spite of all his planning, he forgot team personalities. The skipper and the mechanic couldn't get along and hostilities ensued. A great team needs to work well together and understand their roles and responsibilities.

There was a positive side to my colleague's trip cancellation, however. If they had set sail at that time (September 2001), their GPS system would have been brought down because of the emergency restrictions resulting from the September 11 terrorist attacks in the United States.

➤ Secure Methodology Training

I have attended many seminars in which both project managers and senior executives have disclosed the best and worst features of their respective project management methodologies. One feature highlighted every time is the training of staff on the newly implemented methodology. I have often heard surprised project managers and executives finding out about the "new methodology" on the day it is rolled out.

Table 5.3 Roles and responsibilities in a methodology rollout

Role	Responsibilities	Full-Time	As-Needed
Project sponsor	Provides executive support and is the methodology champion.	✓	
	Encourages and provides feedback to project lead.	✓	
Project lead	Manages the overall implementation of the methodology.	✓	
	Manages the expectations of the client and stakeholders.	✓	
	Ensures that deliverables and milestones are met.	✓	
Business analyst	Identifies all required processes and business requirements.		✓
	Models the methodology of the proposed business model.		✓
	Provides a workflow of the chosen methodology.		✓
Subject matter expert	Provides specialized information on methodologies.		✓
	Sits in all design review methodology sessions.		✓
Computer support	Provides computer hardware and software support.		✓
	Provides architectural design criteria.		✓
Functional managers	Provide input on departmental/regional requirements.		✓
	Assist with resources where needed.		✓
Vendors	Provide software support and integration.		✓
	Assist with integration and acceptance testing.		✓
	Provide usable methodology documentation.		✓
	Provide user training.		✓

There are also many project managers, analysts, engineers, and developers working on project teams in virtually every industry who are inadequately trained in the following areas, which should be part of the methodology training:

➤ Obtaining user requirements.

➤ Building quality into the project.

➤ Configuration management.

It is prudent to notify staff well in advance of the upcoming release or implementation of the methodology. Failure to do so only adds to poor communication. You need to ensure that users understand how the components of the chosen methodology fit together, the types of projects that can be used with the methodology, and the philosophy behind it.

The project lead appointed to head the implementation of a new methodology and processes should include training as part of the entire implementation process. After the methodology is communicated and the workforce trained, companies should encourage their project/development managers to be certified on their new project and/or development methodologies. The following action items must be implemented:

➤ Establish a comprehensive training plan and schedule.

➤ Limit class sizes to 15 members per session.

➤ Identify all project managers and technical leads in the company.

➤ Include computer-based training (CBT) as an option if cost allows.

➤ Provide a conceptual overview and understanding of the methodology.

➤ Provide practical examples.

➤ Discuss processes needed to support the methodology.

➤ Print sufficient color copies of the project methodology for attendees of sessions.

➤ Maintain the necessary electronic files in a centralized repository for easy updates and modification.

➤ Provide annual refresher training to introduce and explain new templates.

➤ How Long Is a Typical Implementation?

Each project methodology has its own unique set of challenges and advantages. Certain methodologies are simply straightforward deployments, whereas others designed from scratch may take longer to deploy. For example, a Commercial-Off-The-Shelf (COTS) method may be simpler to implement than designing a methodology from scratch.

Project methodology implementation durations can range from 8 to 12 weeks for a standard, commercial off-the-shelf package. For a tailored approach, six months is the minimum period needed. A more complex deployment could take substantially longer (e.g., deploying a project methodology in 20 offices globally). Immediate results of implementation of your methodology become evident after a few projects have been completed, but the metrics should be established as soon as possible (i.e., you want to measure the number of projects that succeed in reducing cost or schedule overruns because of the chosen methodology).

➤ Documenting the Project Methodology

During the pilot project, a technical writer or analyst documents the methodology from the initial launch to the completion of the project. This documentation becomes a formalized document or guideline, which is rolled out together with the methodology after it has been accepted by the organization.

➤ Integration of the Methodology into the Business

Simply implementing the new methodology into an existing environment causes problems. The methodology must be integrated without disrupting existing processes and causing the business to come to a stop. The project manager or executive must be sure the new project methodology will provide staff a better way of managing projects.

Be sure that a procurement process is integrated with the relevant methodology at the time the pilot is rolled out—as it is most likely you will need to place orders for project related equipment during this period.

➤ Methodology Infrastructure and Environment

Deciding to implement a project methodology at a moment's notice is like going on vacation in peak season without lodging reservations. Prior planning and upfront confirmation of the environment and infrastructure are essential. Requirements for success include:

- ➤ Establishment of the proper infrastructure and creation of the necessary environment.
- ➤ A centrally located facility where the methodology can be managed.
- ➤ Dedicated software and computer infrastructure to support the needs of the methodology team.
- ➤ Sufficient facilities to accommodate the implementation/ deployment team during the pilot project and postpilot launch.

➤ Implementation Checklist

At Microsoft Corporation, project managers and team leads meet regularly after regular business hours to discuss key software projects. These meetings include aggressive, decisive assessments of tasks and activities to be performed (either for the next day, week, or month). All attendees determine their project priorities and activities. They also formulate and communicate checklists to the necessary team leads.

The project methodology team should ensure that the following questions are answered before launching the chosen methodology:

➤ Do we have all the project templates available in hard copy and soft copy format?

➤ Have we identified all the processes in the organization, and are they relevant?

➤ Have we identified the minimum set of documents needed for the project?

➤ Are the project templates easy to use and identified for use by project phase?

➤ Are templates available online, or are they stored on a server?

➤ Do the templates meet the purpose of the various projects and technology used?

➤ Have we communicated our approach and plan to all stakeholders?

— Road shows to the various departments or regions.

— Brochures circulated before launch.

— Information leaflets circulated to all users.

— Presentations to potential users.

— Involvement of users and subject matter experts.

➤ Are there areas of the business we have not addressed?

➤ Have we considered legal aspects, such as contract management or failure to address legal issues on projects, which could result in lawsuits?

➤ Have we trained users on the methodology?

— By department.

— By selected invitation.

➤ Do we have a technical writer in place to document any changes to the methodology?

➤ Testing the Success of Your Methodology

When the early Romans built an aqueduct, the engineer who designed the structure stood under it when the scaffolding was removed. The engineer's expertise in his craft determined whether he lived or died. The same idea applies to modern day project management. Knowledge of project management matters is imperative for success. If the project fails because of poor methodology or noncompliance, the project manager should be accountable for the failure.

A project manager needs to test and measure the progress of each step of the process. This is achieved by involving the QA department (independent of your project management office) to police or audit your projects on an ad-hoc basis. This results in feedback as to the methodology's use and acceptance in the company. It also shows to some degree how well you are performing.

■ COMMUNICATION

Communication is the backbone of any successful project rollout. Without it, projects have conflict, delays, and failure. Effective communication can be achieved with tools such as an intranet or Web-based technology to inform stakeholders of current status and expected rollout date. Regular briefings with client executives and interaction with the project sponsor are also effective.

➤ Briefings/Presentations

Regular stakeholder presentations are a key part of methodology implementation. The project lead should prepare the following presentations for the client organization:

Kick-off presentation. After the go-ahead has been given for the methodology to proceed, it is necessary to present the (1) aim, (2) scope, (3) team, and (4) deliverables to the client. This presentation communicates the start of the project and gains support from stakeholders.

Informative progress presentations. These presentations are provided to the client at frequent, regular periods (e.g., weekly) to communicate project progress and determine the next steps.

Prelaunch presentation. Before starting the actual launch of the methodology, this presentation involves the staff that will be directly connected with the rollout. Participants may include (1) functional department heads, (2) regional executives, and (3) users. This presentation forms the basis for execution of the rollout. Failure to inform stakeholders would result in miscommunication and possible delays.

Postlaunch presentation. After the methodology has been rolled out to the specific client sites, it becomes necessary to again communicate with the stakeholders to notify them of the success of the rollout. This is the last presentation the project deployment team hosts.

➤ Marketing Campaign

Often, too little is done in a client organization to properly market the implementation of the new methodology. When the implementation team realizes that it hardly addressed the marketing of the methodology, color copies of the methodology are often distributed to the end users. This will not suffice in today's business environment. The project methodology team should have already provided the marketing department or vendor with a proper set of documentation. This documentation should include:

- ➤ Project or development methodology binders describing the methodology, printed in sufficient quantities (and with the ability to get additional copies as needed).
- ➤ Information leaflets for the client organization, or provide the information on the client's intranet.
- ➤ Flashy color brochures depicting the methodology for the internal client departments.
- ➤ Success stories on the value of methodologies posted throughout the organization.

Many companies today generate revenues marketing the adoption and implementation of methodologies to interested clients. They lure clients with their marketing campaigns, which highlight their respective methodologies and provide the justification for having a methodology to support projects.

➤ METHODOLOGY ACCEPTANCE CRITERIA

After the project methodology has been implemented and the first pilot project successfully completed, the project methodology team, together with the client, should walk through the necessary acceptance criteria. Questions to answer include:

- ➤ Has the methodology addressed all areas of our business?
- ➤ Does the methodology allow us visibility to monitor all projects in the pipeline?
- ➤ Have we addressed all necessary templates that are required?
- ➤ Are there quality gates built into our methodology?
- ➤ Will the methodology be able to capture project metrics?
- ➤ If relevant, have the software licenses for the methodology been purchased?
- ➤ Is the hardware in place and in production?
- ➤ Have all the users been provided with methodology training?
- ➤ Have the required support agreements with vendors been approved and implemented?
- ➤ Have the project office team roles and responsibilities been completed?

In the end, the only thing that really counts to the client is the perception of what was delivered and the client experience during the deployment. If the client is happy and well informed, deployment will be easier.

➤ Consider a Pilot Project Deployment

When any project framework or development methodology is implemented, the company should consider deploying a pilot

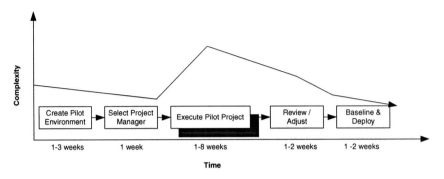

Figure 5.3 Implementation of a pilot methodology.

project before a full-blown methodology rollout. By initiating a pilot project, the project team has the opportunity to prove the effectiveness and true value to the stakeholders. The methodology team then recruits a *pilot project manager* to manage a project using the new methodology. The entire team patiently observes, monitors, and documents all movements in the pilot project.

Any small problems or issues are noted and corrected when the pilot project is complete. The entire team then holds a design review meeting to ensure that any changes are incorporated into the methodology procedures, training, and marketing material. Figure 5.3 shows steps for implementation of a pilot methodology.

■ LESSONS LEARNED

Introduction of any project methodology into an organization requires careful coordination and control. The following are lessons learned on projects rolled out by Fortune 1000 clients:

1. Using a flexible methodology in which projects are approached collaboratively and incrementally provides recognizable results at a much faster pace, compared to an inflexible methodology that forces users to comply with every document and step.

2. Communicate to all stakeholders the status of pilot implementation.

3. Share success and highlights of milestones achieved and benefits that will be gained.

4. You cannot gain acceptance from everybody when deploying a new project methodology; someone will identify missing pieces.

5. Perform an assessment of the organization's current capability, identifying what key process areas need to be improved to gain the maximum benefit; then make the appropriate changes.

6. When working with sales and marketing staff who sell project methodologies to clients, be sure that the project lead is involved before any commitment date is provided as many projects fail when promises are made in isolation by sales teams just to get the contract from a client.

■ QUESTIONS

1. What does *implementing a project methodology into an organization* mean?

2. Name at least four areas of the organization or business that have an impact on the newly implemented methodology.

3. Describe how you would communicate the implementation of a new methodology into an organization.

4. Name five methodology acceptance criteria that are relevant to any methodology implementation.

5. Name at least four job positions that would be required to assist with a methodology rollout.

6. Discuss the importance and contributions of the project sponsor of the new methodology being rolled out.

7. Explain the role of the project office in implementing a project methodology.

8. Why would a project manager consider implementing a pilot before a major methodology rollout?

9. How long is a typical methodology implementation?

■ REFERENCES

Chapman, J. R. "Project Management Scalability Methodology Guide." Available from www.fda.gov/cder/handbook/develop.htm —New Drug Development Process. 1997.

Chapter 6

Supporting the Methodology

Any organization that intends to support a formal project methodology should realize that it would not simply end there. Much more is needed than simply using a project methodology for your project delivery process. You need to support your methodology after you have implemented it. Key factors that your organization should consider before commencing with the implementation include:

➤ There must be an executive commitment to the continual support.

➤ The methodology must be accepted in totality by the organization and all required input must be received.

➤ All project managers and support staff must be trained in the proper use and functionality of the methodology, its tools, and its processes.

➤ All projects must be prioritized and identified in the organization.

➤ Prioritized projects should be funneled through the project office, which, in turn, schedules the projects in accordance with the resources available.

➤ Processes must be updated to reflect the presence of the new methodology (i.e., the financial reporting and executive reporting systems must be updated).

■ LEVELS OF MAINTENANCE

A certain level of support or maintenance must be given to the newly implemented methodology. It cannot simply exist on its own—it requires constant support and nurturing to fully maximize the efforts and value the organization needs. The following levels of support are necessary:

➤ *Level 1: Minor level.* At this level, project templates are updated or removed and replaced by improved versions. A member of the project office team administers this level of support.

➤ *Level 2: Intermediate level.* At this level of support, recommendations to change key processes are considered. A competent member of the project office team who specializes in processes and project management administers this level.

➤ *Level 3: Major level.* At this level, support oversees situations such as a database supporting the framework goes down, project managers do not have access to their files, a phase is added to the methodology, or conformance to a new specification or government regulation requires that the methodology be adjusted. This level of support may generate additional work for the project office team supporting the methodology.

The following questions are frequently asked about the maintenance and support of project methodologies:

➤ When does maintenance begin for a project methodology?

➤ Does the project office maintain the methodology or is this left to individual users?

Maintenance is a fact as business needs change; therefore, although maintenance is necessary at the end of the development process framework definition, it should be considered from the very beginning of the project. The project framework guideline document should make it explicitly clear that support will be provided to all users of the methodology.

A methodology does not ensure maintainability by itself. Maintainability and support are made possible by a combination of five factors:

1. Tools.
2. People.
3. Documentation.
4. Good practice guidelines.
5. A methodology budget.

Guidance on the first three of these aspects can be provided in a methodology framework manual. Good practice guidelines cover aspects such as standards, style guide, use of methodology for the execution of projects, and so on—everything that would have been done automatically for a waterfall approach and should not be forgotten just because a RAD method, for example, is being used.

Methodologies with poor maintainability characteristics are difficult to change and prone to operational problems and errors because they have an adverse effect on the budget. Conversely, methodologies with good maintainability characteristics are quicker and easier to change, are less likely to succumb to problems and errors, have longer lives, and make more effective use of available resources.

■ THE PROJECT OFFICE INFLUENCE

A project office can relieve a project or development manager of the details that can be obstacles to achieving success. It provides centralized management and coordination of multiple projects and resources, as well as establishes a project management culture. Further, a project office can serve as a center of excellence to provide quick and organized access to years of project best practices. Support is the most complex part of the rollout process. The project office must be able to keep track of the complete project portfolio. This includes the selection and prioritization of new projects coming into the organization, as well as cancellation of those that are not meeting the metrics set by the company executives. When a project is in trouble, executives do not want to hear about it only at the last moment. The project office's responsibility is, therefore, to provide a balance or checkpoint for all projects. Additionally, the management of the methodology pipeline is just one aspect of the project office.

➤ Responsibilities of the Project Management Office (PMO)

The project office plays an important part in a methodology. The most logical choice to manage the methodology is the PMO. The relationship between the PMO and the project or development methodologies is shown by the following tasks, which become the responsibilities of the PMO:

➤ Managing the portfolio of projects against the project framework and methodology.

➤ Maintaining the project framework and methodology.

➤ Ensuring that all projects are tracked and measured for performance.

➤ Using tight internal controls to meet company goals and objectives.

➤ Ensuring that best industry practices and standards are constantly applied.

➤ Delegating responsibilities, which should be assigned for the duration of the project.

➤ Participating in cross-functional activities such as QA, finance, and HR.

➤ Monitoring, evaluating, and controlling progress in comparison to project plans.

➤ Ensuring internal company processes are enhanced to support the project portfolio.

➤ Support Tools and Techniques

The PMO supplies all the necessary tools and techniques for use by the company. It maintains the latest versions of these tools and ensures that the most efficient techniques are provided to the project managers working with the project methodology. Table 6.1 lists project support requirements.

➤ Documentation Supporting the Methodology

The saying goes that it's not over until the paperwork is complete. Project documentation forms a crucial part of any project methodology. Each phase requires its own unique set of documentation, which should identify and capture the essence of the project. When a methodology does not have the correct types of documentation and they are inconsistent with the organizational objectives for managing projects, not only are they not used, but they most likely are completed incorrectly. Thus, the project office team has to ensure that the correct documentation is available to the people who use the methodology.

➤ Cost of Supporting a Methdology

Nothing is free, not even maintaining project methodologies. In its simplest form, there may be minimal expenses if the methodology is relatively easy to use. If you have a complex SDLC or an iterative life cycle, the costs to support and maintain such methodologies rise incrementally. Either an internal

Table 6.1 Project methodology support requirements

Support Area	Tools
Planning	WBS tool, templates
Estimating	Cost estimation tools, COCOMO
Project templates	Word processors, spreadsheets, and databases
Project and company process flows	Workflow automation tools

department can maintain methodologies, or this support may be outsourced to an external vendor. In either case, it will cost you money.

Additionally, support costs should be variable based on the priority set by the client demanding the support. This can take many forms, but most often it means that if a client ignores the project methodology guidelines and assigns a higher priority for his or her concern, some cost—possibly an internal charge-back—must be associated.

➤ Auditing the Project Methodology

What are the measures of project success? What are the critical factors that cause projects to be successful or to fail? How useful a measure is project overrun? What contribution has project management made to business performance?

Organization and human issues continue to cause major challenges to the effective implementation of projects. How much new theoretically based research is still to be accomplished is questionable. Organizational learning is an example, however, of genuinely new theoretical ground to explore in the following areas:

➤ Use of tight internal controls to meet goals and objectives.

➤ Use of best practices to ensure success throughout the entire project life cycle.

➤ Delegation of responsibilities, which should be assigned for the duration of the project.

➤ Involvement of cross-functional activities.

➤ Monitoring, evaluating, and controlling progress against project plans.

➤ Achieving Organizational Support

Project managers must be aware that after a project methodology has been implemented, continued support is required from across functional departments in an organization. The project manager in charge of managing the methodology must ensure that a balance exists between the internal and external organizations. Users say that everything is fine until the moment you change their environment (e.g., changing their computer screen). It is, therefore, essential to obtain organizational support from day one.

For example, a large pharmaceutical company such as Johnson & Johnson has many operating companies that require project management services. Cross-functional support and communication is effectively managed on a continuous basis to ensure that no duplication and confusion exists between any operating company project needs. In addition, Johnson & Johnson's project life cycle methodologies are consolidated at all times, and knowledge sharing is encouraged throughout the organization. For this reason, Johnson & Johnson truly stands out as one of the most successful health care companies in the world.

Studies have shown that a clear relationship exists between the number of people-oriented activities and the size of the company, and, more importantly, its organizational culture. This suggests that implementation methodology needs to be based on the characteristics of an organization.

➤ Support Agreements

It is likely that many project offices have integrated tools that are used by all project managers for managing their projects on a daily basis. Companies cannot afford downtime if the software fails. Therefore, it is important that the vendors support the methodology. The support agreements between the support team (i.e., PMO or vendors) should include the following:

➤ Minimum call-back times (e.g., two hours, one day).

➤ Minimum time for the resolution of issues.

➤ Types of resources responding to the types of problems.

➤ Support Infrastructure and Resources

A project methodology and its associated processes, tools, and techniques should be managed from a centralized location in the company. That location should include:

- ➤ Computing support.
- ➤ Remote access support (networking).
- ➤ Facilities (offices).
- ➤ Administration offices.
- ➤ Training facility.

➤ Support Checklist

The project manager should ensure that documentation or deliverables are checked after the company has accepted the project methodology. Be sure that:

- ➤ Service level agreements of all vendors that have systems linked to the methodology are in place.
- ➤ All project templates are in a single repository.
- ➤ A backup exists for all project templates and data.
- ➤ A schedule is in place for regular backups and that the staff is trained to perform the backup procedures.
- ➤ All PMO staff has been trained to answer any questions from project managers in the field (i.e., off-site) or in-house.
- ➤ An escalation process has been communicated to all project managers for problems they may have with the project methodology.
- ➤ A contact list of all project managers and users of the methodology exists.

■ REALITY ON PROJECT SUPPORT

Everything being said, I don't think I can provide enough emphasis on the "political" side of project management. Projects fail for all the reasons I've cited, but they also fail because of poor, or no, management support, competing management philosophies, personal career agendas, and lots of other related reasons that you may have seen, overheard from fellow colleagues, or even personally struggled through. Where are the tools to build project support? Glossy communications just aren't enough. You need to run a project like a political campaign with lots of behind the scenes negotiations and arm twisting to ensure that the metrics by which success will be determined are achieved.

■ LESSONS LEARNED

The following are some valuable lessons regarding support of methodology:

1. Be aware that outsourcing your methodology support to outsiders costs money.
2. Ensure that the organization provides yearly financial support in their budgets for the project office that supports the methodology, improvements, new tools, and so on.
3. Ensure that any SLA for a vendor is approved and signed before anything goes live.
4. Ensure that all project templates are available online and that they work properly.

■ QUESTIONS

1. Why do we talk about support for a project methodology? Is support really necessary?
2. Who owns a project methodology in an organization? Is it the project office, the program office, an external vendor, or the users? Explain.
3. Name at least three areas of support that likely would be needed when supporting a project framework in an organization?

4. Do you agree that different levels of support are needed in an organization to tend to the overall methodology? (Is it a fixed dedicated team or managed ad hoc?)

5. Who maintains the methodology after implementation?

6. Describe how you, as the newly appointed manager, would begin to address the support of an enterprisewide project management methodology. You have to present a plan of action to ensure that the company project managers have a reliable framework. Looking at the files, you notice that two vendors who currently provide limited online support deployed the project methodology. Various people in your company review project templates intermittently, and users have stated that the templates don't always work.

Chapter 7

Project Templates
and Techniques

■ ESTABLISHING A TEMPLATE ROAD MAP

Templates—also referred to as *artifacts* or *boilerplate templates*—
are essential to the success of any project. Templates are seldom found bundled together nicely in a box, ready for use.
Project or development managers do not want to spend the
time to create new project templates for their projects. Instead,
they benefit greatly from using a wide variety of tried and
tested methodology templates, which gives them time to concentrate on the actual project.

This chapter provides a reliable source of useful methodology templates that might be required by project or development
managers during specific project phases. Whether managing
projects or actually developing the technical detail (i.e., design
or build phase), you will face constant change. Methodology
templates support the user in creating and maintaining project data/information in a formalized and structured manner.
Templates also focus on guiding users to specifically define key
deliverables, addressing issues such as quality, scope, resources,
risk, and cost. These templates help project team members
gain a better understanding of the project and its associated
tasks. Table 7.1 lists advantages and disadvantages of project
templates.

Table 7.1 Advantages and disadvantages of project templates

Advantages	Disadvantages
Reusable—no need to start from scratch	Needs custom tailoring
Saves time	May contain difficult style and ineffective format
Pick and mix	
Ease of use—simply edit, copy, and paste	
Format already exists	

Although the lightweight methodology family discussed in previous chapters does not encourage large amounts of project documentation, it requires some methodology templates.

■ TEMPLATE SELECTION

I recently bought a pair of snow boots from the Timberland Web site. After selecting the boots, I was immediately offered accompanying winter socks—an excellent way to cross-sell something I had not planned to purchase. Likewise, when choosing a methodology, you would surely need some templates to accompany it. After you have defined the methodology, add the appropriate methodology templates (e.g., concept phase would require a business case template and a feasibility template). However, you must be very selective with project templates, as there are essentially hundreds of forms, checklists, and templates you could use. If you select every template, you've created a monster. Select too few, and you are short. Through extensive experience on many different projects, I offer a complete project template toolkit which is available on my personal website www.jasoncharvat.com/sales.html. This toolkit can be used with any project methodology and for each project, you merely identify and select the relevant templates you need.

Figure 7.1 shows that each stakeholder in the project plays an important role. Sometimes, stakeholders require a complete set of templates for their tasks. Other times, a stakeholder needs only specific templates (e.g., QA stakeholders require QA-related documentation).

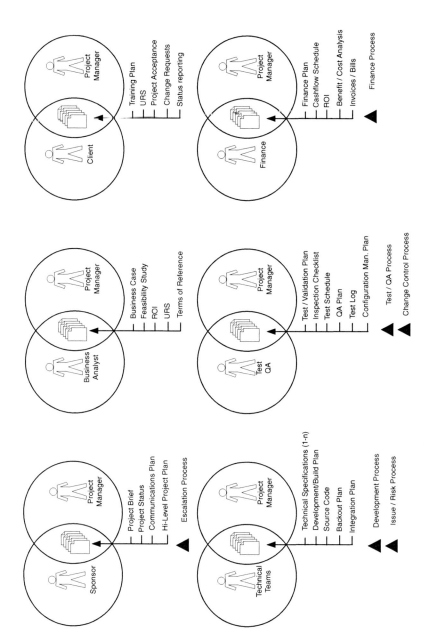

Figure 7.1 Project templates per project role.

➤ Purpose of Project Templates

The definitions and templates found in this book are best described as *generic* because certain methodologies and companies may have their own variations of the templates they need. Therefore, project templates should be modified based on the specific methodology to be used or tweaked to suit your company standards. Figure 7.2 provides a summary of the contents of the CD-ROM that I provide on my website. Once you obtain the CD-ROM, there are 120 different project templates available for use. The structure is listed in possible phases you could expect to encounter on a typical project. If you have just started your project, you would open the *Concept Phase* folder and locate the relevant template.

■ CONCEPT PHASE TEMPLATES

➤ Master Record Index Template for Project Start

The master record index is used at the start of a project. It lists all documents used during the initial phase of the project and indicates status of the documents (i.e., approved or not approved). The master record index assists in auditing and provides project managers with a quick reference of documents required for the project. This is a one-page document and the template is simple to complete.

➤ Feasibility Report Template

The feasibility report is a formal report that provides the findings of the feasibility study, which is undertaken before the project starts. The report includes an overview of the request, the reasons for initiating the project, the findings of the study, recommendations either for going forward or for rejecting the request, and the estimated cost and effort of the project. If available, it also summarizes the expected advantages to the group (e.g., cost savings, less maintenance effort) of the new deliverable.

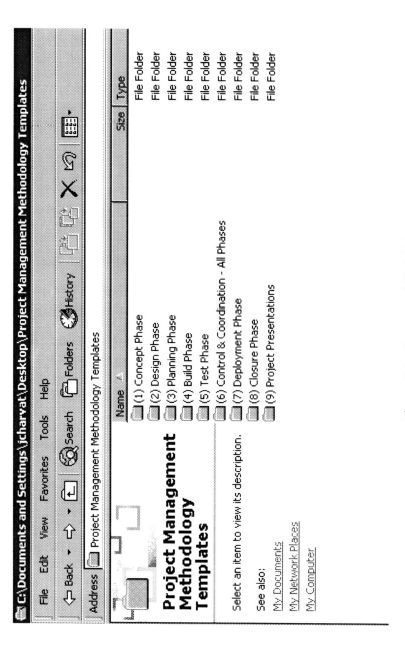

Figure 7.2 Contents of CD-ROM.

201

➤ Product Brief Template

The product brief document describes the aim, benefits, and objectives of the proposed product. It could describe the development of a new photocopier, satellite, or medical drug. Additionally, it establishes the parameters for the work to be done, including tasks to be performed (scope) and tasks not to be performed (outside of the scope of the project). It may include expected deliverables, risks, the project team and their roles, and measures of success (close-out criteria).

➤ Product Plan Template

The product plan document describes where the product will compete, development time line, scope, and resources.

➤ User Requirements Specification (URS) Template

The URS document describes, in business terminology, the client's project requirements. Many failed projects have had either no or poorly documented user requirements. The client should typically complete the URS, but this does not always happen. In any event, be prepared to complete this template for the client, because the URS sets the entire direction of the project. Without a URS in place, you may encounter clients asking for more than what was originally bargained for. The URS usually precedes a system requirements specification document. To ensure that the URS template is properly completed, engage the client in a series of discussions, questionnaires, or workshops to obtain the requirements (see Figure 7.3).

➤ Financial Analysis Spreadsheet Template

The financial analysis spreadsheet calculates the various financial benefits and value of your project. It provides the necessary information to guide you in estimating costs.

➤ Request for Proposal (RFP) Template

The RFP is a formal document soliciting proposals from selected vendors. Included in this document is a description,

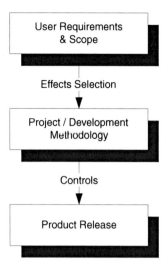

Figure 7.3 Importance of URS on projects.

usually detailed, of the project. Also specified is the format that the vendor proposal must follow, which allows the requestor to compare one vendor's response to another's. An RFP template varies from company to company.

➤ Statement of Work (SOW) Template

The SOW is a formal, signed document, which describes the project needs and the solution. The following sections may be included in the SOW:

- ➤ Executive summary, which summarizes the project at a high level.
- ➤ Project scope (including assumptions).
- ➤ Solution (approach to take).
- ➤ Roles and responsibilities of each individual (and/or company) on the project team.
- ➤ Closeout criteria (agreed-to deliverables, which define when project is complete).
- ➤ Pricing (project costs may be a separate document).

➤ Discovery Template

The discovery template is a document used by the project team when a client requests the team to perform a "discovery" of the client's current business environment and explore future intended business state. As the template name implies, it is an exploratory document. It should contain a road map of the technology used, processes, resources used, anticipated growth, and direction to take. This template requires some innovative input.

➤ Project Charter Template

The project charter is a high-level document generated by the project manager to provide an overview of the project and to inform senior stakeholders and sponsor of the project initiative.

➤ Project Roles and Responsibilities Template

Project managers use the roles and responsibilities template to illustrate the various roles to be played on the project. It specifies the responsibilities of each member of the project team. Without this template, communication would be difficult because project team members would be unsure of task responsibility on the project.

➤ Project Issue List/Log Template

The project issue list or log is a document that identifies all issues requiring resolution. Each issue is categorized with degree of severity and priority and/or date for resolution. If the issue is deemed a risk to the successful and timely completion of the project, it is transferred from the issue list to the risk list.

➤ Project Risk List/Log Template

The project risk list or log is a document used to identify all conditions or events that may endanger the project's timely and successful completion. Each condition is labeled with a degree of severity and probability of occurrence. Actions to mitigate the risk should be included.

➤ Project Management Plan (PMP) Template

The PMP is similar to a project definition report (PDR). The PMP is one of the most important documents in any project manager's template toolkit and needs to be completed as quickly as possible. It defines the project scope, objectives, interfaces, resources, budget, and schedule. The PMP document can also consist of appendixes containing data on related topics, such as communication and quality assurance.

➤ Project Definition Report (PDR) Template

The PDR is a formal document generated at the project definition workshop (PDW), which usually includes the project sponsor, the project team, and the immediate stakeholders of the project. The aim of the PDR is to clarify and define the purpose, scope, and final objectives of the project. It serves to introduce the team to the stakeholders as well as generate commitment from all. Additionally, the document must contain a clear description of the domain of the project, the problems to be solved, and the final goals to be achieved.

➤ Terms of Reference (TOR) Template

The TOR documents the "rules" that project participants must follow. This document includes the vision, mission roles and responsibilities, project goals, budget, project control and QA processes, and escalation procedures, among other factors. It is prepared specifically to describe goals, activities, and scope of work to be undertaken. It should also provide an outline for the business plan, prototype site, evaluation, and readiness. The TOR should usually be limited to 10 to 15 pages.

➤ Business Case Template

The business case is an important document used to address not only the effect of investments but also the processes that ensure that capital spent on projects brings an exceptional, risk-adjusted return. The goal of the business case is to define the opportunity and reasons that management may accept the undertaking of a systems development or enhancement project. These business case objectives and descriptions, therefore, provide the basis for the business assessment. This document is a key decision-making document for not only the company executives, but also investors and other important stakeholders. Additionally, many top executives that read business cases today demand substantially more than cut-and-paste work. Project managers must strive to find those opportunities that increase top- and bottom-line performance, and methods to improve cash flow and free up working capital.

➤ Feasibility Study Template

The feasibility study is used to determine if the proposed project is practical and will meet the needs of the group requesting the project. The study includes analysis to determine the practicality of the project and a formal report detailing the findings and recommendation. A business analyst, consultant, or executive familiar with the proposed solution usually completes the project feasibility template.

➤ Team Contract Template

The team contract is a formal document developed by the project manager describing the project in terms of a *team* contract, which is then signed by all parties to the project. It solidifies the project and brings the team together.

➤ Project Contact List Template

The project contact list shows all members of the project team, including the sponsor. The list includes contact information, such as phone number, pager number, location, and primary and backup contacts, including their roles on the project.

➤ Project Brief Template

The project brief defines the aimed scope of the project. It is simple to complete and well accepted by project team members. All stakeholders are identified in the project brief.

➤ Project Status Report Template

The project status report highlights project accomplishments since the last reported status. It is used to identify outstanding issues and may include specific action items requiring resolution. The status report should include upcoming activities with their associated dates. Depending on the required report, it may also be necessary to include financial and schedule information such as planned versus actual. The status report should be concise.

➤ Risk Management Plan Template

The risk management plan includes the risk event, the probability of risks, and the consequences of these risks. Recommendations and actions to be taken on the project are included. The risk management plan should be approximately 5 to 15 pages, depending on the project size.

➤ Work Breakdown Structure (WBS) Template

The WBS is the blueprint used to carry out the work. It identifies the actual tasks to be performed and the hierarchal relationships of the tasks. It also defines the task duration and the anticipated resources in the project. Favored by many project managers, the WBS differs from project to project, but the breakdown is usually limited to four levels or fewer.

➤ Project Agenda Template

The project agenda document is used by project staff to plan required project meetings. The agenda sets the direction of the meeting by listing specific agenda items. Each agenda item should have a specific time allocated to it so that all items will be covered.

➤ Project Kickoff Meeting Template

The kickoff meeting document lists the essential requirements for conducting a kickoff meeting. The kickoff meeting allows project stakeholders to gain a better understanding of project objectives, time frames, and resources.

➤ Minutes of a Meeting Template

The minutes should be recorded at all project meetings. Minutes of meetings should be short and concise and state the actions, due dates, and responsibilities by party. The minutes of a meeting should be sent to participants and interested parties within 48 hours of the meeting. A simple e-mail template can be used to summarize the project meeting minutes in bullet format with action items and completion dates; then send the e-mail minutes to your distribution list. Although a small percentage of project/development managers in companies I have worked with actually distribute minutes of the meeting, and forms are an essential part of the project communication process.

■ DESIGN PHASE TEMPLATES

➤ Technical Specification Template

A technical specification document is needed because it formalizes the technical details of the project. It should detail the development methodology to be followed for the solution. The technical manager of the project should work in conjunction with subject matter experts (SMEs) or vendors to create the required technical specification documents. There can be more than one technical specification, depending on size and complexity of the project. For example, you could have billing, software, and integration specifications just for one project. The technical specification document can be formal (e.g., for heavy-weight methodologies) or informal as a workflow or software code (e.g., for lightweight methodologies).

➤ Provisional Implementation Plan Template

During the initial phases of the project, the provisional implementation plan document should be used to start planning the implementation of the project.

➤ Provisional Back-Out Plan Template

Developing a project back-out plan is rarely considered in many project organizations today because those involved assume the project will succeed. However, only 16.2 percent of projects succeed; thus, 83.8 percent fail. A back-out plan is necessary because the initial project plan may not be successfully launched or it may fail because of technical difficulties. The backup plan, which should describe a safe, alternative route, then takes effect.

➤ Functional Specification Template

The functional specification is a technical document, usually prepared by the development team. It describes the user requirements in technical terms in preparation for system development.

➤ Master Record Index Template—Design Phase

This index lists all the documents that are required during the design phase of the project. This is a good way to keep track of the approved documents in each phase—you can readily open the project binder and determine which documents were approved and used during the design phase.

➤ Resource Allocation Template

The resource allocation document can be used by a project manager to document all resources (team) working on the project. It helps manage the resources' time over the entire project. This useful template allows monitoring of percentage of resources' time and monthly costs to the project.

➤ Provisional Service Level Agreement Template

The provisional service level agreement sets out the necessary levels of support needed for the project after it is deployed. The provisional service level agreement defines the services needed and states to what extent they will be met.

➤ Deviation/Concession Template

The deviation template is a formal document used by the project team to indicate any deviation from the original scope of the project. It signifies that a deviation has been made and that all parties agree to the change.

➤ Actual Cost Spreadsheet Template

The actual cost spreadsheet is useful when a project manager would like to capture actual costs of the project—staff, equipment, suppliers, and associated costs.

■ BUILD PHASE TEMPLATES

➤ Master Record Index Template—Build Phase

This index lists all the build phase documents that may be required by the project during the build phase. It helps keep track of the approved documents for each phase; you can readily open the binder and quickly determine which documents were approved and used during the build phase.

➤ Acceptance Testing Template

Acceptance testing is performed by the QA team to test and accept the solution that has been built before release to the client. Many clients have their own acceptance testing staffs, who need to be included in the development of any acceptance testing documents.

➤ Test Plan Template

The test plan lists specific situations or events (test cases) to test for functional (incorrect logic) or interpretation (miscommunication at the design stage) errors. Test cases and expected results are prepared before the test phase.

➤ User Acceptance Test (UAT) Plan Template

The UAT document lists the specific business requirements (test cases) to test the business logic and flow of the solution. This includes testing to ensure the system meets the business needs (tests against the business requirements).

➤ Development Testing Template

This document, which tests for functionality and stability, may be performed at (1) a module or program level and (2) a system level, which also tests the interaction between modules or programs (operational test procedures).

➤ QA Error Log Template

The QA error log is used to record all errors on the project after finalization by the deployment team. The error log lists all errors found by the QA team and should include specific examples of how and when the errors failed during the test process. Until all the errors have been resolved, the product or solution cannot be delivered to the client.

■ IMPLEMENTATION PHASE TEMPLATES

➤ Master Record Index Template— Implementation Phase

This index lists all the implementation phase documents required by the project during the deployment phase. A quick look at the binder will determine which documents were approved and used during the deployment phase.

➤ Implementation Plan Template

The implementation plan is a formal document that identifies the steps for deploying the solution into the designated environment. The plan includes all project tasks that must be completed, the responsibilities of identified stakeholders, deliverables, and completion dates. Additionally, when relevant, the implementation plan should contain any resources such as hardware, software, machinery, logistics, connectivity, project staff, and cost for each item required to implement the target solution.

■ CLOSURE PHASE TEMPLATES

➤ Master Record Index Template—Closure Phase

This index lists all the closure documents that are actually needed on the project during the closure phase.

➤ Postproject Review Template

The postproject review template is used to start a review after the project has been deployed. This review should capture the inputs and reviews of the client, team members, and sponsors.

➤ Support Plan Template

The support plan is a crucial project document that must clearly and accurately describe (1) the what, (2) the how, (3) support time, and (4) who will provide the required support needed after the project is handed over to production or operations. It also requires specific metrics and details to support the solution.

➤ Sign-Off Certificate Template

The sign-off certificate is a formal document approved by key stakeholders who authorize the acceptance and satisfactory completion of their areas of the project. This document usually requires only a few pages.

■ SELECTING PROJECT TEMPLATES

It is senseless to use every project template for your project. You merely add a great administrative burden on yourself, and you will likely end up over schedule because of it. For example, it is inefficient to use the entire arsenal of templates on a database migration project. Instead, you should selectively identify critical templates required by the business. The following types of projects require different levels of project templates:

➤ *Small-sized projects.* These are projects ranging from one to four months in duration. The emphasis is on completing the project as quickly as possible. Examples are small migration projects, creation of a Web site, or simply upgrading.

➤ *Medium-sized projects.* These projects take up to twelve months in duration, which is the norm in most companies. They are not quickly resolved and usually consist of external vendors and integration. The level of risk and change control starts increasing with medium-sized projects. Examples are development of (1) a new network center in a new location, (2) a cellular phone project, and (3) a business intelligence project.

➤ *Super-sized projects.* These are the largest of all projects. They may take a few years to complete. Examples of these projects are the development and building of ships or space vessels, large construction projects, or development of a new drug.

Figure 7.4 shows three categories of projects (i.e., small, medium, super) and the minimum project templates that are recommended. For small projects, the emphasis is on having only the minimum project templates, medium-sized projects require a few more, and the super-sized projects require the

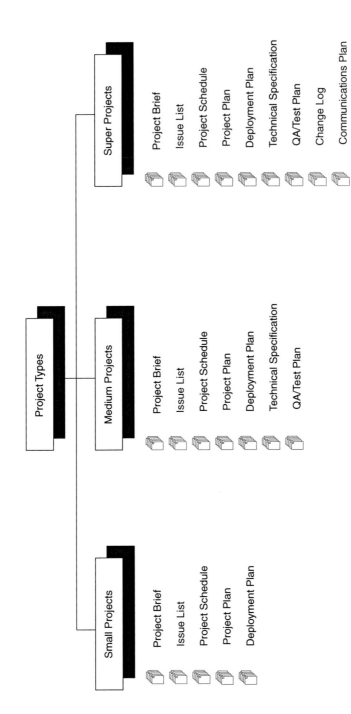

Figure 7.4 Minimum number of templates needed per project size.

most, because of the amount of communication and coordination required.

➤ Template Checklist

The project or development manager should ensure completion of the following steps:

- ➤ All templates have been identified for each phase.
- ➤ Templates have been cross-referenced against available methodology standards used in the organization.
- ➤ Resources have been identified to complete the templates.
- ➤ Templates are accessible for use.
- ➤ Templates are available in hardcopy format.

➤ Format of Project Templates

Project templates should be provided in a standard electronic format. Many companies use the most common word processing or spreadsheet packages, such as MS Word or MS Excel. The formatting of the templates usually undergoes a series of editing checks and technical reviews before distribution. Text sufficient to guide the user should be included on each project template. The PMO should also maintain and publish a separate master record index with a complete list of all project templates in circulation in the company. The master record index should contain the following information:

- ➤ The project template name.
- ➤ Current revision number.
- ➤ Date issued for use.

■ LESSONS LEARNED

As a new project manager for a client, I was responsible for developing certain project documents. From previous experience,

I knew that these templates were available online at a specific Web site; I was not fully aware that the templates came at a price. Because I didn't want to recreate anything already available, I obtained approval to purchase these templates, which took too long. The lesson learned: Identify and secure the necessary templates well ahead of time.

■ QUESTIONS

1. What is the importance of project templates? Discuss.

2. Name five project templates used in the concept or initiation phase of a project.

3. What is the purpose of a *project brief/project definition report?*

4. Discuss three ways to access templates in an organization. Assume you are a new project manager.

5. Explain whether it is necessary to use all templates for your project.

6. Explain how to select specific templates when assigned a project by your organization (e.g., business case, ROI). Would you discuss it with your project sponsor or take the initiative yourself?

7. List eight essential project artifacts or templates you would use for a 30-month project, which is awaiting approval by an executive board. The project will design and build a state-of-the-art electric vehicle, with participation from three well-known manufacturers. You are the project manager. State which type of methodology you would recommend.

Chapter 8

Project Processes and Trends

■ PROCESS CONSIDERATIONS

Looking beyond your company's portfolio of projects—products and services that it works so hard on—reflect on those core processes needed to support overall objectives. Beyond being passionate and committed in your work, there must be a fundamental focus on having the right processes in place. There will always be opportunities for you as project or development manager to tailor processes; therefore, you must understand how and when processes come into play. Someone once said, "We don't use standard business processes; we have unconventional ways of recharging our entire business, which totally support our project and development methodologies."

On any project you undertake, you may encounter situations from which you need to remove certain processes because they are not in your project scope. For example, you don't need to do financials on your project (on many projects, project managers don't touch finances). In this case, you would drop the financial process and use the rest. Or, you are using a Waterfall methodology on a project and your client insists on document management (i.e., version control, distribution). In this case, you need to add this process to the project scope. Project methodologies:

➤ Demonstrate the ability to get the job done.

➤ Meet certain criteria set by auditing or certification groups monitoring the company.

➤ Allow the company to prioritize resources accordingly, based on the project's progress.

➤ What Is a Process?

A *process* is best defined as who (is doing what), where, when, and how to reach a certain goal (see Figure 8.1). Because processes are the foundation of successful projects, it is important to develop those processes that reflect the organization's unique strengths and work patterns. In project-oriented organizations, project management serves as the core process, which integrates the development/deployment practices to complete projects successfully. The use of project methodologies is the most significant factor in project management today.

Methodologies impose a disciplined process on the project life cycle with the aim of making the execution and completion more predictable and more efficient. This is done by developing a detailed project framework with a strong emphasis on

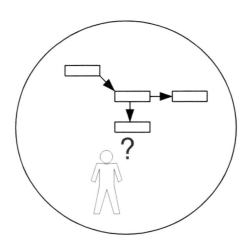

Figure 8.1   What is a process?

other project areas such as planning, design, procurement, finance, acceptance testing, and so on (see Figure 8.2).

➤ What Core Processes Are Available?

Core processes are typically those key processes that transform "what the company does" into valuable outputs for its client. Without these key process areas in place, projects would struggle to meet their schedules. Table 8.1 lists those key processes, which any company should consider using.

Decide which processes you need on the project. You could use either all of them or only a selected few. However, they need to be available and ready to execute when a project manager wants them. Companies that are ISO certified or regulated by groups such as the FDA or CMM often have their processes in place, which implies that these companies have defined key processes across the organization and their staff are familiar with them.

Project management processes have been around for years, but have never been fully integrated into the project management "space" or ecosystem. Recently, processes have been reemphasized through changing technology and commercially available methodologies that necessitate leveraging

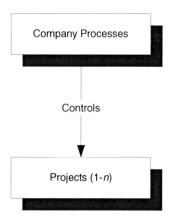

Figure 8.2   Effect of processes on a project.

Table 8.1   Key process areas

Processes	Area Addressed	Resource Needed
Change control	Configuration management	Configuration manager
Procurement	Purchasing of equipment	Procurement manager
Issue and risk	Problems on the project	Project manager
Documentation	Document management	Configuration clerk
Estimation	Project cost forecasting	Cost estimator
Communication	Project communications	Project manager
Recruitment	Hiring new project resources	Human resources /personnel
Marketing and sales	Marketing and sales	Marketing and sales manager
Project framework	Actual project methodology	Project manager
Finance	Budgeting and invoicing	Financial manager
Audit	Project	Quality assurance
Quality assurance	Project quality	Quality assurance manager
Training	Training	Trainer
Product development	Developing/manufacturing	Development manager

all processes, which were possibly never fully used before. However, organizations have been slow to adopt them because most off-the-shelf processes are too generic to work effectively.

■ DEFINING AN EFFECTIVE PROCESS

An effective process is a process that helps organizations move rapidly through their activities, reducing risk and forming a common standardized approach for all to follow. Table 8.2 lists some of the key factors of an effective process, which creates a stream of advantages for companies.

Table 8.2 Key factors for defining processes

Provides guidelines for efficient development of quality systems and solutions.
Reduces risk and increases predictability.
Captures and presents best practices.
Promotes a common vision and culture for the organization.
Provides a roadmap for applying tools and techniques.
Easy to understand and simple to use.

➤ Demystifying Some Crucial Questions

The project or development manager, at this stage of defining processes, should ensure that the following questions have been answered before starting a project:

➤ Have I determined which processes will be used on my project?

➤ Have I appointed team members to develop those processes?

➤ How long will it take to complete?

➤ What templates do I need to create for these processes?

➤ Do any steering committees or teams need to be established?

■ OBSERVATIONS FROM THE TITANS

Exasperated by multimillion-dollar cost overruns and delays measured in years, a growing number of large corporations are taking an innovative approach to systems development. Sometimes the opportunities that exist mean that you need to reconfigure the existing business model.

In the past two years, American Express Financial Advisors, Inc., United Air Lines, and Ryder Systems, Inc., have all established project management offices because they must manage their methodologies on a regular basis. These offices have the sole mandate and authority to authorize changes in systems development deadlines and budgets. They act as the security check for catching any projects in the red. This is the way effective companies work.

Nynex Corp., meanwhile, requires all outside vendors working on Nynex IS projects to comply with the telecommunications company's project management methodology. Tracking a project's progress against its initial goals not only helps keep a development project on track, but also helps IS measure and document productivity, according to Richard V. Mulcahy (2001), staff director of IS at the company. He said:

> When processes were manual, it was easy to measure IS productivity. If you automated payroll, you'd lose 30 clerks. So it was easy to prove IS's worth. Now that we've squeezed out most of the fat from the organization, we need to move to improved project management efficiency.

When American Express Financial Advisors set up its project office, budget overruns of as high as 500 percent were not uncommon at the Minneapolis-based company, according to Warren G. Herreid (2001), a former lieutenant in the military and the office's senior director. Most increases resulted from changes in project requirements and/or development tools. Two years ago, for example, a mid-project switch from Windows operating system to OS/2 caused a 200 percent overrun and more than a one-year delay on a general ledger application. Now, all project change requests with a price tag of more than $250,000 must be approved by a technology council and Herreid's office, which supports more than 70 active projects and a 750-person IS organization. This is a methodology in place that works.

Productivity has increased 40 percent since United Air Lines created its four-person, San Francisco-based IS project office, according to Richard L. Gleason (2001), project office manager. Currently, the office supports 17 major development projects. It also maintains an online electronic library containing all project deliverables, schedules, and documentation. Gleason said:

Before the project office, the planning that got done had the depth of a back-lot facade you see at Universal Studios. Now we have a very standardized way of planning projects with a financial aspect tied in to track how we are doing against those plans. (p. 2)

➤ Case No. 1: Norigen Communications Inc.

It's been a year since Norigen Communications Inc. of Toronto arrived on the scene as a competitive local exchange carrier, offering a range of communications services to businesses across Canada—a year of massive growth from 15 to 500 employees and several key acquisitions.

Managing that magnitude of growth is never easy, acknowledges Allan McNeely (2001), Norigen's director of program management; but with a strong corporate commitment to project management behind it to keep the company on track, business continues to thrive.

The powerful thing about what we're doing here at Norigen is the way we're set up. We have a formal program management office where we handle not only all of our projects, but we also handle the processes . . . Project Management gets into every aspect of the business—it's absolutely full spectrum. (p. 1)

Under McNeely is a team of nine project managers who execute specific projects in specific departments. If a project spans multiple departments, that project is termed a *program* and is handled by a program manager charged with the task of pulling it all together. One reason for the group's success is that company president and COO Bill Baines throws "170 percent support" behind the concept, said McNeely. Another is that it breaks down the communication barriers between departments, building a more collaborative and efficient work environment. McNeely continued:

The biggest thing project management brings to the table is to help a company stop looking at itself as a functional matrix, the classic silos (departments) of doom where you have information randomly popping out of the top. Some lands in the next silo but a lot lands in between and just rots away. (p. 2)

Instead, a project management focus helps a company align itself horizontally so that information from departments is shared. "They don't fly the plane, but they have a view of what's going on across all of the projects," he says. It's a model he has seen in other companies during the course of his research in the area and one he prefers to others.

In a June 1999 report designed to find ways to improve IT project management, Shevlin concluded that although companies were managing IT projects well, they were not achieving results. The problem he identified was that more emphasis was being placed on the process of managing the project than on the application or product being built. To help shift the focus back to the product, Shevlin advises dividing project office teams into two groups: product managers and project managers. Product managers focus on the business reasons for doing the project while project managers focus on the process itself.

Finding good candidates, however, isn't easy. McNeely, who interviews people daily, says:

> It is a challenge to find people who are real project managers. There are a lot of folks out there who have the title project manager or project coordinator, but they're not really professionally trained project managers.

► Case No. 2: City of San Diego

Facing the challenges of running more than 160 IT projects concurrently at any given time, the city of San Diego hired RCG Information Technology to set up a project office to establish formal project management policies, tools, and methodologies appropriate for the city's structure. RCG IT was selected for the job because they were flexible in the way they implemented a truly effective project solution, by aligning the city's IT projects with the selected project methodology. Richard Wilken (2002), director of IT&C, said:

> Our IT projects are sometimes not successful or vary significantly project to project. We needed help bringing our

house in order as far as establishing strong and clear accountability for project management in the organization and improving project delivery, project management practices, and communication overall.

➤ Experiences with CMM

Some organizations have seen tremendous benefits using a CMM approach. Motorola Transmission Products, transitioning from a Level 1 to a Level 2 organization, had the following experience:

- ➤ They went from having great difficulty predicting ship dates to predicting schedules within 15 percent of baseline.
- ➤ They formerly could not measure quality before the product hit the field and had to fix products after delivery to customers, but the CMM approach helped them control quality and limit field problems to less than two per month.

Raytheon Equipment Division transitioned from a Level 1 to a Level 3 organization, and they found that the following was achieved:

- ➤ A $7.70 return on every dollar invested in process improvement.
- ➤ A $4.48 million savings over six projects in one year.
- ➤ A 140 percent increase in productivity.

According to Bill Pollak (2001), public relations manager for the Software Engineering Institute (SEI) at Carnegie Mellon University, where the Capability Maturity Model was developed, there are two general kinds of metrics for software development—metrics that focus on management, such as CMM, and metrics that focus on technical practices and performance such as lines of code written and function point analysis (a tool for measuring changes in functionality from software development projects). These metric standards do not compete and the performance metrics are part of a later stage of the CMM model. Watts Humphrey (1989), creator of the Capability Maturity Model, claims that Microsoft could have saved $4 billion in development costs with proper quality processes and better testing procedures.

■ PROJECT METHODOLOGY PROCESSES

As discussed in earlier chapters, the necessity for having solid project processes in place remains undisputed. Some of these essential project processes are:

- ➤ Issue management process.
- ➤ Risk management process.
- ➤ Change control process.
- ➤ Procurement process.
- ➤ Planning process.
- ➤ Estimating process.
- ➤ Quality assurance process.

Figure 8.3 shows the various levels that company processes affect. For example, in the financial process, which has a ripple effect throughout any project, the internal financial process for issues such as estimating, quoting, invoicing, credits, and disbursements should be understood before starting a project.

■ ISSUE MANAGEMENT PROCESS

An *issue* is something that has happened that can threaten the success of your project. With issue management, you encounter typically four different scenarios:

- ➤ Unconscious issues (there, but unknown).
- ➤ Conscious issues (not publicly known, although discussed with the right people).

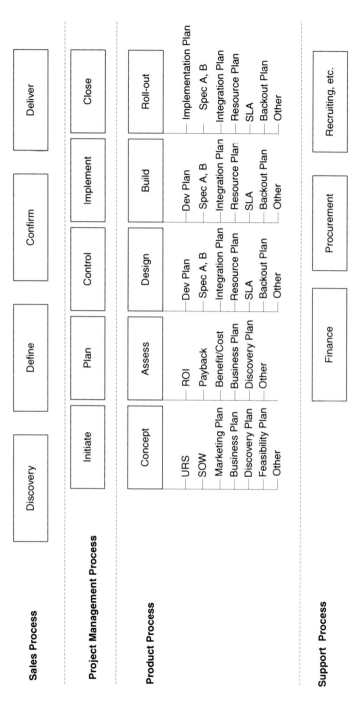

Figure 8.3 Integration of process areas on a project.

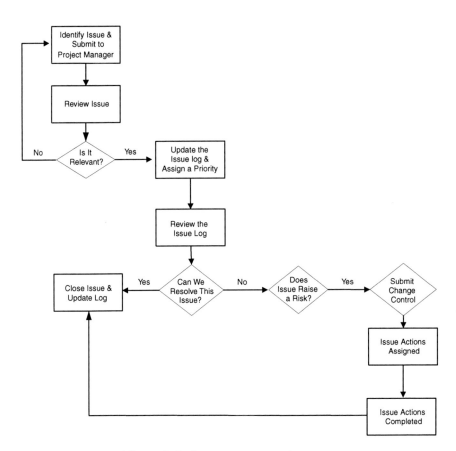

Figure 8.4 Issue management process.

➤ Shared issues (shared but remain unresolved).

➤ Shared and resolved issues (the ideal scenario). (See Figure 8.4.)

The issue process is key to the successful delivery of any project. It ensures that each issue identified in the project environment is documented, prioritized, and resolved in an appropriate length of time. Issues cannot remain unresolved for an indefinite time. For the purpose of your project, you need to follow an issue management process. Start by tackling issues first. Concentrate on:

- ➤ Identifying current issues.
- ➤ Identifying themes among the issues (e.g., vendor issues, financial issues).
- ➤ Clarifying the issues.
- ➤ Prioritizing the issues (e.g., priority 1, or color code red, yellow, green).
- ➤ Selecting the issue you want to work on.
- ➤ Understanding why the issue exists.
- ➤ Selecting a solution with an action item(s).

Issue management is introduced to this project through the implementation of five key processes. A formal process for the:

1. Identification of project issues.
2. Logging and prioritization of project issues.
3. Determination of issue resolution actions.
4. Monitoring and control of assigned issue resolution actions.
5. Closure of project issues.

➤ Raise Issue

This process provides the ability for any member of the project team to raise a project-related issue. The following procedures are undertaken:

- ➤ Issue originator identifies an issue applicable to a particular aspect of the project (e.g., scope, deliverables, time scales, organization).
- ➤ Issue originator completes an issue form and distributes the form to the project manager.

➤ Register Issue

This process allows the project manager to review all issues raised and determine whether each issue is applicable to the project. This decision is based primarily on whether the issue impacts:

➤ A project deliverable specified in the project deliverables register.

➤ A quality deliverable specified in the quality plan.

➤ The time scale specified in the project plan.

If the project manager considers the issue appropriate to the project, a formal issue is raised in the project issue register and an issue number is assigned. The project manager assigns an issue *priority* based on the level of impact of the issue to the project.

➤ Assign Issue Actions

This process involves the formal review of the issue register by the project review group. The project review group reviews each issue in turn (based on issue priority) and may decide to:

➤ Close the issue in the issue register if there are no outstanding issue actions and the issue is no longer impacting the project.

➤ Raise a change request if the issue has resulted in the need for a change to the project.

➤ Raise a project risk if the issue is also likely to impact the project in the future.

➤ Assign issue actions to attempt to resolve the issue.

➤ Implement Issue Actions

This process involves the implementation of all actions assigned by the project review group and includes:

➤ Scheduling each action for completion.

➤ Implementing each action scheduled.

➤ Reviewing the success of each action completed.

➤ Communicating the success of each action completed.

➤ Issue Roles and Responsibilities

Define the roles and responsibilities for all resources (both within and external to the project) involved with the identification, review, and resolution of issues in the project. There are three primary roles when working with project issues. They are:

1. *Issue originator.* The issue originator initially identifies the issue and formally communicates the issue to the project manager. The issue originator is formally responsible for:

   — Identification of project issues.

   — Documenting the issue, using the issue log.

   — Notifying the project manager of the new issue.

2. *Project manager.* After the project manager receives, records, monitors, and controls the progress of all issues in a project, he or she is responsible for:

   — Receiving all issues raised by the person identifying the issue(s) and determining that they are relevant to the project.

   — Recording all issues deemed appropriate to the project in the issue register.

   — Prioritizing all issues in the issue register and initiating the project review group meeting.

   — Reporting and communicating all decisions made by the project review group.

   — Monitoring the progress of all issue resolution actions assigned.

3. *Project steering group.* The project steering group determines the issue status and assigns issue resolution actions where appropriate. The steering group is responsible for:

   — Regular reviews of all issues recorded in the issue log.

   — Identifying issues that require change requests and/or project risks to be raised.

   — Assessment of the status of issues listed in the issue log.

—The closure of issues that have no outstanding actions and are no longer impacting the project.

➤ Issue Log

The issue log is the main log in which all issues are registered and tracked through to resolution. See the accompanying CD-ROM for the issue log template.

■ CHANGE CONTROL PROCESS

When we speak about change control, then I have to address the whole issue of scope creep, both on the end user's side and on the developer's. The business plan (should) define the value that will result from the expenditure of money and resources. This value definition needs to be translated into specific measurable requirements that then become the functional specifications for the developers. Then the change management process can track the impact of new insights and understandings as the project matures without losing scope of what it was that was originally determined to have enough business value to warrant the project in the first place.

A change management process should control changes in any project environment affecting products or services being developed by the project team. A core change team must assess the impact of any proposed changes to gauge cost, schedule, documentation, and training, plus the change's impact on re-tooling implications. The change management process identifies, defines, evaluates, and approves these changes before any implementation. This configuration management process must be introduced to the project, through the implementation of five key formal processes for:

1. Submission and receipt of change requests.
2. Review and logging of change requests.
3. Determination of the feasibility of change requests.
4. Approval of change requests.
5. Implementation and closure of change requests.

Figure 8.5 provides an overview of the change processes and procedures for effectively managing project-related change.

➤ Submit Change Request

This process provides the ability for any member of the project team to submit a request for change to the project. The following procedures are completed:

➤ Change requestor identifies a requirement for change to any aspect of the project (e.g., scope, deliverables, time scales, organization).

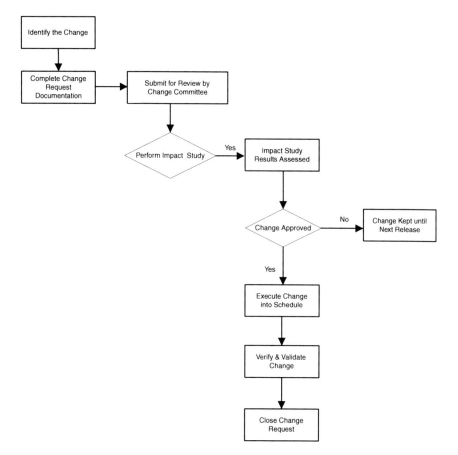

Figure 8.5 Change control process.

➤ Change requestor completes a change request form (CRF) and distributes the form to the change manager. The CRF provides a summary of the change required, including the:

—Change description.

—Reasons for change (including business drivers).

—Benefits of change.

—Costs of change.

—Impacts of change.

—Supporting documentation.

➤ **Review Change Request**

This process allows the change manager to review the CRF and determine whether a full feasibility study is required for the change approval group to assess the full impact of the change. The decision is based primarily on the:

➤ Number of change options presented.

➤ Complexity of the change options requested.

➤ Scale of the change solutions proposed.

The change manager opens a change request in the change log and records whether a change feasibility study is required.

➤ **Identify Change Feasibility**

This process involves the completion of a full change feasibility study to ensure that all change options have been investigated and presented accordingly. The change feasibility study involves definition of the:

➤ Requirements.

➤ Options.

➤ Costs and benefits.

➤ Risks and issues.

➤ Impact.

➤ Recommendations and plan.

A quality review of the feasibility study is then performed to ensure that it has been conducted as requested and the final deliverable is approved and ready for release to the change approval group. All change documentation is then collated by the change manager and submitted to the change approval group for final review. This documentation includes:

➤ The original change request form.

➤ The approved change feasibility study report.

➤ Any supporting documentation.

➤ Approve Change Request

In this process, the change approval group formally reviews the change request. The change approval group chooses one of the following outcomes regarding the change proposed:

➤ Reject the change.

➤ Request more information related to the change.

➤ Approve the change as requested.

➤ Approve the change subject to specified conditions.

The change decision is based primarily on the following criteria:

➤ Risk to the project in implementing the change.

➤ Risk to the project in *not* implementing the change.

➤ Impact to the project in implementing the change (time, resources, finance, quality).

➤ Implement Change Request

This process concerns the complete implementation of the change, which includes:

➤ Identifying the change schedule (i.e., date for implementation of the change).

➤ Testing the change before implementation.

➤ Implementing the change.

➤ Reviewing the success of the change implementation.

➤ Communicating the success of the change implementation.

➤ Closing the change in the change log.

➤ **Change Roles**

In this process, the roles and responsibilities for all resources (both within and external to the project) involved with the initiation, review, and implementation of changes in the project are defined. For example:

➤ The *change requestor* initially recognizes a need for change to the project and formally communicates this requirement to the change manager. The change requestor is formally responsible for:

—The early identification of a need to make a change to the project.

—The formal documentation of that need, through the completion of a change request form.

—The submission of the change request form to the change manager for review.

➤ The *change manager* receives, logs, monitors, and controls the progress of all changes in a project. The change manager is formally responsible for:

—Receiving all change requests and logging those requests into the change register.

—Categorizing and prioritizing all change requests.

—Reviewing all change requests to determine if additional information is required to present the submission to the change review group.

—Determining whether a formal change feasibility study is required to complete a change request submission.

—Initiating the change feasibility study, through assignment of the change feasibility group.

—Monitoring the progress of all change requests to ensure process timeliness.

—Escalating all change request issues and risks to the change approval group.

—Reporting and communicating all decisions made by the change approval group.

➤ The *change feasibility group* completes formal feasibility studies for change requests issued by the change manager. The change feasibility group is formally responsible for:

—Performing research to determine the likely options for change, costs, benefits, and impacts of change.

—Documenting all findings in a change feasibility study report.

—Performing a quality review of the report and approving the report for submission.

—Forwarding the report to the change manager for change approval group submission.

➤ The *change approval group* determines the authorization of all change requests forwarded by the change manager. The change approval group is formally responsible for:

—The review of all change requests forwarded by the change manager.

—The consideration of all supporting change documentation.

—Approving/rejecting each change request based on its relevant merits.

—Resolving change conflict (where two or more changes overlap).

—Resolving change issues.

—Determining the change implementation timetable (for approved changes).

➤ Project Change Steering Group

Regarding the project environment, it is necessary that the project change steering group schedule, carry out, and review the implementation of all changes in a project. The change implementation group is formally responsible for:

➤ Scheduling of all changes (subject to the general time frames provided by the change approval group).

➤ Testing of all changes before implementation.

➤ Implementation of all changes in the project.

➤ Review of the success of a change, following implementation.

➤ Request for closure of a change in the change log.

■ RISK MANAGEMENT PROCESS

The risk management process is fundamental to the successful delivery of any project—whether it is light or heavyweight in nature. The risk management process is there to ensure that each risk is properly identified, documented, categorized, and resolved within the project environment. For the purpose of this project, *risks* are defined as "those project events that are most likely to adversely affect the ability to produce the required deliverables." Therefore, to understand risk management at its best, an overview of five key processes that make up the risk management framework follows:

1. Identification of project risks.
2. Logging and prioritization of project risks.
3. Determination of risk mitigating actions.
4. Monitoring and control of risk resolution action items.
5. Closure of project risks.

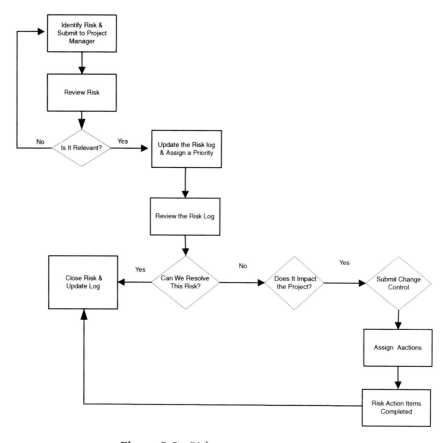

Figure 8.6 Risk management process.

Figure 8.6 provides an overview of the risk processes and procedures, which are undertaken by project managers or executives to effectively manage any project-related risks.

➤ Raise and Assess the Risk

This process provides the ability for any member of the project team to raise a project-related risk. The following procedures are followed:

➤ The originator identifies a risk applicable to a particular aspect of the project (e.g., scope, deliverables, time scales, or organization are in jeopardy).

➤ The originator completes the risk log and distributes the form to the project manager. (See the accompanying CD-ROM for a risk log template.)

➤ The project manager ensures the risk is captured accurately.

➤ The project or development manager reviews all raised risks and determines whether each risk is applicable to the project.

➤ The project or development manager formulates an impact of the risk.

If the risk is considered relevant by the project or development manager, a formal risk is raised in the risk log, where the impact and probability are calculated, based on the input provided by the person originating the risk.

➤ Assign Risk Actions

The number of people to assign to risk-related tasks depends on the size of the project. On small to medium-sized projects, the project manager usually performs this task with limited help. On super projects, it is not uncommon for a dedicated project risk steering group (two to four people) to be created. In this case, the steering group would obtain and formally review all submitted project risks and either (1) approve, (2) reject, or (3) postpone until further assessment has been completed. Options that the steering group would present to the project or development manager would be one of the following:

➤ Close the risk in the risk log if there are no outstanding risk actions and the risk is no longer likely to impact the project.

➤ Submit a change request to resolve the risk, thereby indicating that the project will have a change.

➤ Assign action items to resolve the risk.

➤ Executing and Resolving Risk Items

After logging the risks into the risk log, the project or development manager needs to move forward and resolve these risks.
The best way to achieve this is to:

- ➤ Start scheduling each risk on the project—use the proj-
  ect schedule.
- ➤ Define who on the project or externally would be work-
  ing to resolve the risk.
- ➤ Execute each risk as scheduled.
- ➤ Review or test the successful execution of the risk.
- ➤ Document and communicate the success of the risk just
  resolved.

➤ Roles and Responsibilities—PROJECT RISK

The Originator

The originator of the risk is the most important person in the
chain of events. The originator is someone on the project
team—or sometimes externally—who initially identifies the
risk and formally communicates the risk to the project manager. The originator is responsible for:

- ➤ Identifying the risk.
- ➤ Logging the risk.
- ➤ Submitting the risk or risk log form to the project/
  development manager.

Project or Development Manager

The project manager is the central person throughout the entire risk process. He or she receives, documents, and monitors
the status of all risks during a project life cycle. The project or
development manager is responsible for:

- ➤ Assessing risks submitted for relevance to the project at
  hand.

➤ Recording accurately in the risk log.

➤ Presenting the risk to the risk steering group or sponsor for review.

➤ Assessing the risk using SMEs to gain more detail.

➤ Communicating the decision to implement or reject the risk.

➤ Implementing the risk into the project.

➤ Monitoring the report on its successful completion.

Project Steering Group

The project steering group is a team that formally reviews all risks—usually on super projects—and confirms what the probability and impact to the project would be. A risk could have severe cost and schedule impacts, which the project or development manager may not have considered. The steering team assigns steps or action items to resolve all known risks. The steering team is formally responsible for:

➤ The regular review and audit of all project risks recorded in the risk log.

➤ Ensuring that the risk process has been followed to mitigate risks raised.

➤ Recommending risk action items.

➤ Bringing closure of all risk items on the project.

■ ASSEMBLING A CORE PROCESS TEAM

By this stage, you have been bombarded by processes, forms, templates, and methodologies, which you can use in your company or for your own project(s). This can be very unsettling to any practicing project manager who does not have the time to spend on creating new processes.

The solution to that problem is to assemble a core team of specialists to drive the development or enhancement of the necessary processes for the company. As the business model changes, so must its processes change. The following team should be brought together to ensure that all areas of the business and project work together:

➤ Process leader or champion.

➤ Quality assurance representative.

➤ Project office manager representative.

➤ Ad-hoc members from the required process groups.

■ SUMMARY

This book's mission—to inform you about methodologies—was intended primarily to comfort the methodology-afflicted and afflict those pushing their own methodologies as the be-all-and-end-all of methodologies. Throughout this book, you have seen the need for a tailored approach to building your projects. Different projects require different methodologies—including templates and processes. Occasionally, a new idea comes along that makes us reexamine our philosophy on methodologies—this new idea is the concept of the lighter, faster, agile family of methodologies. My advice: When you are faced with a small project, consider using these new methodologies.

Additionally, we discussed the similarities of project processes in many companies; those processes used on projects—irrespective of their industry type—are largely universal in nature. After all, a change process is a change process. It may be tweaked a little on a certain project, but it remains basically the same. We also saw numerous project management methodologies available for use, depending on the application, project size, technology, and schedule. Therefore, select the most appropriate one, identify your processes, and get on with it. The key is to manipulate and configure things to suit your environment.

■ QUESTIONS

1. What is a *process?*
2. List five processes you would likely encounter when following a project methodology.

3. Discuss the importance of taking organizational processes into consideration. Assume you have to purchase equipment. Would you adhere to the company procurement/solicitation process or would you create your own procurement process?

4. How would you address the scenario when a certain process takes too long? How would you deal with this situation?

5. Who owns organizational processes?

6. When dealing specifically with a change management process, how would you ensure that proposed change requests are incorporated in your project and how would the change control process assist the project?

7. Discuss the *gate* process. Is this purely a quality-driven process or something more?

8. What is the purpose of an issue management process?

9. What is the purpose of a risk management process?

■ REFERENCES

Gleason, Richard L. United Air Lines Project Office IT report, 2001.

Herreid, Warren G. Personal communication, 2001.

Humphrey, Watts. *Managing the Software Process.* Boston: Addison-Wesley, 1989.

McNeely, Allan. Project communications, 2001.

Mulcahy, Richard V. Project communications, 2001.

Pollak, Bill. Project communications, 2001.

Shevlin, R. IT project IT report, 1999. p. 2.

Wilkin, Richard. "San Diego calls on RCGIT to Improve Project Delivery." Available at http://www.rcgit.com/news/pr9-11-01.389.cfm, 2002.

Appendix

Questions and Answers

Following are the end-of-chapter questions, along with suggested answers. I welcome your critique.

■ CHAPTER I

Questions

1. Define the concept *methodology*.
2. List five shortcomings of a project methodology.
3. Apart from a project management methodology, what other methodologies would be considered relative to the project?
4. What do we mean by *project management methodology* and *project framework?*
5. What does the term *project strategy* mean? Is it the same as a business strategy?
6. How would you explain the benefits of adopting a project methodology to your client or organization?
7. Does the type of organizational structure affect the efficiency by which projects are managed through the methodology?

Answers

1. *Methodology* is a set of guidelines or principles that can be tailored and applied to a specific situation. In a project environment, it can be a list of things to do. This could be a specific approach, templates, forms, and even checklists used over the project life cycle.

2. Shortcomings of a methodology are:

   ➤ Many of the project life cycle methodologies are abstract and high level.

   ➤ There are insufficient narratives to support these methodologies.

   ➤ They are not functional nor do they address any operational areas (i.e., QA, CM, testing).

   ➤ Many of the methodologies simply ignore the industry standards.

   ➤ Many methodologies are simply incomplete.

3. Other methodologies relative to a project methodology in an organization include (1) recruitment methodology, (2) development methodology, (3) support methodology, and (4) marketing methodology.

4. A *project framework* is more inclusive than methodology because it has templates, processes, project techniques, and training. Product management methodology is the process used to get from point A to point B.

5. *Project strategy* is specific and focused on the project to be executed and deployed; it is based on a specific set of objectives and project scope. Without a project strategy, it is unlikely that the project would be planned very well. A *business strategy* is more comprehensive from an organizational perspective, which focuses on embracing IT, marketing, sales, manufacturing, and HR and the ability to forge ahead of its competitors.

6. You should be able to convince clients that adopting a project management methodology is an effective technique used to guide projects through the design and deployment

of a product or service. It provides an organized and consistent process for approaching a project, and it provides templates and checklists to project teams.

7. Yes, an organizational structure does play a key role in the manner in which projects are identified, ramped-up, executed, and managed to full conclusion. Certain structures, such as a matrix structure, which requires project managers to work across functional silos, are more complex. A simpler approach in which organizations create project teams, formed to drive home company strategy, results in a stronger project structure.

■ CHAPTER 2

Questions

1. Define the term *project life cycle*.
2. Methodologies are the best weapon in a company's arsenal if they want to avoid what?
3. List five reasons that projects fail and state what possible solutions could prevent failure.
4. What does the term *project strategy* mean? Is it the same as a *business strategy*?
5. What are the five levels of the capability maturity model?
6. List three reasons why team members would dislike methodologies?

Answers

1. A *project life cycle* is a collection of project phases. Project phases vary by project or industry, but some general phases include (1) concept, (2) development, (3) implementation, and (4) support.
2. Methodologies provide companies the opportunity to avoid inconsistency and nonstandardization throughout the organization when managing their projects.

3. The following typical failures occur on projects:

➤ Incorrect or no choice of methodology. *Solution:* Assess what the correct methodology should be.

➤ Poor estimation. *Solution:* Spend additional time estimating the project with a cost accountant or estimating tool.

➤ Poor planning. *Solution:* Use planning techniques and templates with the project team.

➤ No change control. *Solution:* Implement a change control process on the project with regular checks and assessments for each change.

➤ Poor implementation. *Solution:* Consider the type and scale of implementation that is required.

4. *Project strategy* is specific and focused on the project to be executed and deployed; it is based on a specific set of objectives and project scope. Without a project strategy, it is unlikely that the project would be planned very well. A *business strategy* is more comprehensive from an organizational perspective, which focuses on embracing IT, marketing, sales, manufacturing, and HR and the ability to forge ahead of its competitors.

5. The five levels of the capability maturity model are initial, repeatable, defined, managed, and optimized.

6. Team members dislike for methodologies are: (1) Methodologies are a waste of time; (2) They don't represent what really happens on a project; and (3) They don't reflect the actual detail technical requirements for executing the project.

■ CHAPTER 3

Questions

1. Name five objectives when selecting an enterprisewide project management methodology.

2. What is the difference between a *project methodology* and a *development methodology?*

3. If you evaluate your project with the client and he or she states that the project took too long, do you think that a standard waterfall approach was a probable cause? Discuss.

4. Name five best practices for selecting or deploying project methodologies.

5. Discuss the rationale that *one* methodology does not fit all projects.

6. Is PRINCE2 suitable for non-IT projects?

7. What does the term *project strategy* mean? Is it the same as a *business strategy?*

Answers

1. Objectives when selecting an enterprisewide project management methodology include:
   - ➤ Overall company strategy—how competitive are we as a company?
   - ➤ Size of the project team and/or scope to be managed.
   - ➤ Priority of the project.
   - ➤ How critical is this project to our company?
   - ➤ How flexible is the methodology and its components?

2. A *project methodology* is the entire structure used to support a project. It consists of templates and processes and is the generic standard for all projects used in a company. A *development methodology* is specific to the technology and is more technical in nature.

3. Today, many methodologists think the waterfall methodology is the dinosaur of all methodologies. The waterfall methodology could be a probable cause for a project's running over schedule. Possibly a RAD or iterative approach would deliver results sooner.

4. Five best practices for selecting or deploying project methodologies are:
   - ➤ Use standard-proven processes and techniques.
   - ➤ Draw on best industry practices and trends.

> ➤ Use standard best practices to reduce everyday project problems.

> ➤ Look at implementation time and cost reduction.

> ➤ Minimize templates and administration.

5. There is not one universal methodology that will suit all projects. Depending on the type, complexity, and completion date of the project, it may be necessary to assess the type of methodology needed.

6. Yes, PRINCE2 can be used for non-IT projects.

7. *Project strategy* is specific and focused on the project to be executed and deployed; it is based on a specific set of objectives and project scope. Without a project strategy, it is unlikely that the project would be planned very well. A *business strategy* is more comprehensive from an organizational perspective, which focuses on embracing IT, marketing, sales, manufacturing, and HR and the ability to forge ahead of its competitors.

■ CHAPTER 4

Questions

1. When dealing with a waterfall methodology, can one proceed with the life cycle if the requirements have not been finalized and signed off on by all parties?

2. Define *heavy* and *light* methodologies.

3. Name the benefits of iterative development on a project.

4. Explain how you would convince your client or organization of the benefits of adopting a project methodology.

5. Does the type of organizational structure affect the efficiency by which projects are managed?

6. List five reasons that most projects fail today.

7. Based on your answers in the previous question, would a project methodology resolve these failures?

8. Describe the difference between the spiral and waterfall methodologies.

Answers

1. No, a waterfall methodology requires or emphasizes that one phase needs to be completed before the next phase begins. If the user requirements are incomplete, the subsequent phases become extremely complex, which is likely to result in schedule and cost overruns.

2. *Heavy* methodologies are predictive in nature, which results in many unsuccessful projects. A heavy methodology takes time; the design and deployment are dependent on each other. *Light* methodologies are more agile and adaptive in nature. They focus on being more informal, yet communicative. Light methodologies are designed and built face-to-face so that information flows more freely and swiftly than a heavy methodology would.

3. The benefits of iterative development on a project are:

➤ It encourages user feedback.

➤ The system grows by adding new functions to each development iteration.

➤ Misconceptions are identified upfront.

➤ Continuous testing is performed throughout the project.

➤ Allows for lessons learned on previous iterations.

4. The benefits of adopting a project methodology include: (1) it adds value to the business in terms of repeatable standard, (2) it provides a uniform way for projects to be managed, and (3) it provides a platform to introduce quality and planning into the project.

5. An organizational structure has a direct effect on the manner in which projects are staffed, equipped, and managed through the chosen life cycle. Large organizations with many departments working in a matrix or functional structure may take longer to complete than a project structure with everyone assigned by project rather than by department.

6. Most projects today fail because of:

➤ Poor communication.

➤ Poor estimation.

➤ Improper deployment.

➤ Ineffective user requirements.

➤ Poor change control.

7. Yes, a project methodology adds value to projects where no methodology is present. A methodology is not a silver bullet that excuses poor planning and deployment; instead, it guides the team on proper techniques and checklists, which will negate many of the obstacles found on projects today.

8. The waterfall methodology is the most common methodology found today. It is linear in approach—most tasks are sequentially aligned to the previous and next tasks. The spiral methodology iterates the processes of planning, designing, building, testing, and delivering, until the system is ready to be released to the client.

■ CHAPTER 5

Questions

1. What does *implementing a project methodology into an organization* mean?

2. Name at least four areas of the organization or business that have an impact on the newly implemented methodology.

3. Describe how you would communicate the implementation of a new methodology into an organization.

4. Name five methodology acceptance criteria that are relevant to any methodology implementation.

5. Name at least four job positions that would be required to assist with a methodology rollout.

6. Discuss the importance and contributions of the project sponsor of the new methodology being rolled out.

7. Explain the role of the project office in implementing a project methodology.

8. Why would a project manager consider implementing a pilot before a major methodology rollout?

9. How long is a typical methodology implementation?

Answers

1. Implementing a project methodology into an organization demands a dedicated team to research and deploy a new manner in which projects will be managed.

2. The organization may be impacted by the implementation of a new project methodology in the following areas of business:
   ➤ Financial.
   ➤ Procurement.
   ➤ Training.
   ➤ Human resources and/or recruitment.

3. Communicate a new methodology though (1) a series of methodology deployment presentations to project and functional managers, (2) hold methodology training classes, (3) hand out information flyers, or (4) have senior executives endorse the new methodology throughout the organization.

4. Acceptance criteria that need to be established for a typical project methodology implementation are:
   ➤ Has the methodology addressed all areas of our business?
   ➤ Does the methodology allow us visibility to monitor all project pipelines?
   ➤ Have we addressed all necessary templates that would be required?
   ➤ Are there quality gates built into our methodology?
   ➤ If relevant, have all the software licenses of the methodology been purchased?

5. Job positions required to assist with a methodology rollout are project lead, business analyst, sponsor, and process engineer.

6. The project sponsor provides executive support, champions the methodology, and provides guidance to the project team on the implementation and necessary objective feedback.

7. The project office plays a key role with any project implementation. If it is a new implementation, the PMO will

assist with the deployment of the methodology into the organization until it is fully operational and then resume with postimplementation.

8. A pilot project allows a team to assess the results of the methodology on a smaller scale instead of implementing a full-blown methodology rollout that might fail.

9. A typical methodology implementation depends on the size of the organization and the company's project maturity level; but usually a basic implementation takes between 8 and 12 weeks.

■ CHAPTER 6

Questions

1. Why do we talk about support for a project methodology? Is support really necessary?

2. Who owns a project methodology in an organization? Is it the project office, the program office, an external vendor, or the users? Explain.

3. Name at least three areas of support that likely would be needed when supporting a project framework in an organization.

4. Do you agree that different levels of support are needed in an organization to tend to the overall methodology? (Is it a fixed dedicated team or managed ad hoc?)

5. Who maintains the methodology after implementation?

6. Describe how you, as the newly appointed manager, would begin to address the support of an enterprisewide project management methodology. You have to present a plan of action to ensure that the company project managers have a reliable framework. Looking at the files, you notice that two vendors who currently provide limited online support deployed the project methodology. Various people in your company review project templates intermittently, and users have stated that the templates don't always work.

Answers

1. After a project management methodology has been established in a company, it needs to receive proper support and maintenance. This involves ensuring constant monitoring of the entire framework ecosystem, which includes the project methodology, templates, processes, information systems, resources, and facilities.

2. The project management office must own the project methodology. A centralized body in the company must be accountable for managing the methodology. Any problems encountered can be efficiently resolved and communicated to project managers. There are then also those organizations that dislike PMOs and consider them as a non-billable function and therefore considered overhead.

3. Project support can be categorized into three main areas of support, namely:

   ➤ *Level 1 support:* Basic support that must be resolved within two hours.

   ➤ *Level 2 support:* Intermediate support that must be resolved within one day.

   ➤ *Level 3 support:* Advanced support that has to be resolved within one week.

4. First, you would need to assess the situation and solicit valuable input from project managers, executives, and project staff as to the shortcomings of the enterprise project methodology. You should concurrently assess the current project tools, techniques, training, and processes being used and then formulate a recommendation with an action plan. This is to be presented to the company executives, recommending the support needed, including the support agreements that need to be put in place to get the methodology back on track.

5. Either the QA or the PMO department can maintain the methodology, depending where it is located. It really depends on the organization.

6. To support any methodology, you need to understand the size and complexity of the methodology (i.e., complex

waterfall or open source methodology), the number of users, and which components of the methodology were being used at which times. This could imply that you may need to support project templates or processes, provide continuous training to the users, and upgrade existing methodology software tools. It is wise to establish a service-level agreement with the organization or project teams to provide a support model for them.

■ CHAPTER 7

Questions

1. What is the importance of project templates? Discuss.
2. Name five project templates used in the concept or initiation phase of a project.
3. What is the purpose of a project brief/project definition report?
4. Discuss three ways to access templates in an organization. Assume you are a new project manager.
5. Explain whether it is necessary to use all templates for your project.
6. Explain how to select specific templates when assigned a project by your organization (e.g., business case, ROI). Would you discuss it with your project sponsor or take the initiative yourself?
7. List eight essential project artifacts or templates you would use for a 30-month project, which is awaiting approval by an executive board. The project will design and build a state-of-the-art electric vehicle, with participation from three well-known manufacturers. You are the project manager. State which type of methodology you would recommend.

Answers

1. The purpose of project templates is to assist project managers or business executives in a productive manner, with

already-prepared document frameworks, ready for completion with specific project deliverables.

2. Templates used in the concept phase are URS, SOW, RFP, business case, and feasibility study.

3. The purpose of the project brief or project definition report is to define the aim, scope, objectives, and deliverables of the project to be undertaken.

4. Project templates should be readily accessible to project managers through one of the following channels:

   ➤ On the company network residing on a common directory.

   ➤ On a company intranet site.

   ➤ In stand-alone CD-ROM format.

5. When working on a project, it is not necessary to use every project template available. Instead, identify with the key stakeholders which templates are necessary for the type and size of project. Smaller projects require fewer templates than larger projects.

6. When deciding on project templates, it is necessary that the project manager identify which templates are needed. After compiling a list of templates needed, the list should be reviewed with the project sponsor. The sponsor provides the necessary input, which should formalize the minimum number of templates to use. By following this approach, the project sponsor is involved.

7. Although each project can be approached differently, I would employ an SDLC methodology because more coordination is needed between all the various parties (i.e., designers, technicians, inspectors, marketing managers), who may reside globally. My choice of templates for this size project is:

   ➤ Project brief.

   ➤ Project feasibility report.

   ➤ Business case.

   ➤ Statement of work.

   ➤ Technical specification.

➤ Quality assurance plan.
➤ Communications plan.
➤ Contact list.

■ CHAPTER 8

Questions

1. What is a *process?*
2. List five processes you would likely encounter when following a project methodology.
3. Discuss the importance of taking organizational processes into consideration. Assume you have to purchase equipment. Would you adhere to the company procurement/solicitation process or would you create your own procurement process?
4. How would you address the scenario when a certain process takes too long? How would you deal with this situation?
5. Who owns organizational processes?
6. When dealing specifically with a change management process, how would you ensure that proposed change requests are incorporated in your project and how would the change control process assist the project?
7. Discuss the *gate* process. Is this purely a quality-driven process or something more?
8. What is the purpose of an issue management process?
9. What is the purpose of a risk management process?

Answers

1. A *process* is a flow of key inputs and outputs performed by various company resources, to reach a certain goal.
2. The following processes are likely to be encountered on a project:
   ➤ Procurement process.
   ➤ Change control process.

➤ Issue process.

➤ Risk process.

➤ Financial process.

3. Accommodating existing organizational processes for a project is mandatory because processes affect the outcome of project deliverables. Assuming we have to order equipment on the project, it may be possible that the company has no existing procurement process in place to order and take receipt of this equipment. In this instance, you have to develop a procurement process at the start of your project. If the company has a procurement process in place, you would need to assess the lead times for equipment ordering and delivery. It is not uncommon for many projects to face a few weeks' delay in purchase order approvals. This will affect the project dramatically. Therefore, project managers need to assess each required process before project commencement.

4. For any process that takes too long, an assessment needs to be performed to determine lead times, and you need to facilitate the necessary changes to speed up the process by amending the existing process—implementing a project waiver or deviation.

5. The quality assurance team in a company contains the most qualified members to accurately define, document, and maintain each process used by the company on their projects. It is best that they be centrally seen as the owners of company processes. This team will subsequently delegate business representatives to be subowners of their respective processes (e.g., the financial manager is accountable for the efficiency of the financial process used on projects).

6. Any change to the project should be captured in a standardized change control process. This implies that the proposed change and its impact on the project—in terms of cost, technology, schedule, and so on—should be recorded from the change requests into a change log.

7. The gate process is a review process, which guides the project team through the various project phases, ensuring the status of the project deliverables.

8. The purpose of the issue process is to identify, document, and resolve all known project issues, thereby ensuring that the project does not fail. Each issue is tracked according to its severity and high-impact issues are escalated as risks.

9. The purpose of the risk process is to identify, document, and resolve all risks on the project.

Index

About the Author

Jason (Jay) Charvat is an accomplished project management consultant, who has extensive international experience in the systems engineering and information technology fields. He has completed many successful projects in the defense, logistics, manufacturing, publishing, governmental, pharmaceutical, cellular, and telecommunications industry verticals. He has extensive knowledge on business optimization—portfolio management, project methodologies processes, and practical techniques used in the completion of projects. He is a certified business consultant and has consulted regularly throughout the United States. He is a member of the Project Management Institute (PMI). He holds a B.Sc. (Information Sciences) degree, as well as numerous professional qualifications from the United Kingdom (London). He has served as a commissioned Air Force captain specializing in the information technology, armament, and avionics environments. Jay serves as a project management consultant and senior manager for RCG Information Technology, Inc., in New Jersey, where he is assigned to Johnson & Johnson as project manager. Jay is also the author of *Project Management Nation: Goals for the New & Practicing IT Project Manager*. He is a contributing writer for CNET networks. He can be reached at info@jasoncharvat.com or www.jasoncharvat.com.

Lightning Source UK Ltd.
Milton Keynes UK
UKOW02n1617310516

275336UK00001B/26/P